T0360852

The Customer Experience Model

For any company, defining the most efficient marketing concept to create a competitive customer experience (CX) is vital for sustained development. The focus of this research is the creation of a comprehensible practical approach to the development of client experience: the Customer Experience Model (CXM).

The practical application of the CX model will allow companies to create value for their customers and key stakeholders, thus generating the necessary profit and building conditions for further development. Balancing academic research and real-world applications, *The Customer Experience Model* provides a framework that readers can understand and utilize to implement improvements in a company. In this work the readers also will learn about application in customer experience formation of such concepts as "systems thinking", "learning organization", and "Lewinian Experiential learning cycle". The role of a leader in the formation of an effective customer experience will be shown as well. Also, the readers will get an obvious idea of how to plan customer experience and measure its effectiveness.

The Customer Experience Model shows the latest state of knowledge on the topic and will be of interest both to students of business schools and universities at an advanced level, academics and reflective practitioners in the fields of leadership, organizational studies, marketing, and strategic management and consulting.

Adyl Aliekperov is a Leadership and Strategy Consultant.

Routledge Focus on Business and Management

The fields of business and management have grown exponentially as areas of research and education. This growth presents challenges for readers trying to keep up with the latest important insights. Routledge Focus on Business and Management presents small books on big topics and how they intersect with the world of business research.

Individually, each title in the series provides coverage of a key academic topic, whilst collectively, the series forms a comprehensive collection across the business disciplines.

Public Relations Crisis Communication
A New Model
Lisa Anderson-Meli and Swapna Koshy

Implicative Marketing
For a Sustainable Economy
Florence Touzé

Global Entrepreneurship Analytics
Using GEM Data
Milenka Linneth Argote Cusi and León Darío Parra Bernal

The Customer Experience Model
Adyl Aliekperov

Organizational Justice and Organizational Change
Managing by Love
Dominique A. David

For more information about this series, please visit: www.routledge.com/Routledge-Focus-on-Business-and-Management/book-series/FBM

The Customer Experience Model

Adyl Aliekperov

Routledge
Taylor & Francis Group

NEW YORK AND LONDON

First published 2021
by Routledge
52 Vanderbilt Avenue, New York, NY 10017

and by Routledge
2 Park Square, Milton Park, Abingdon, Oxon, OX14 4RN

Routledge is an imprint of the Taylor & Francis Group, an informa business

© 2021 Taylor & Francis

Library of Congress Cataloging-in-Publication Data
Names: Aliekperov, Adyl, author.
Title: The customer experience model / Adyl Aliekperov.
Description: New York, NY: Routledge, 2021. |
Series: Routledge focus on business and management |
Includes bibliographical references and index.
Identifiers: LCCN 2020018619 | ISBN 9780367478254 (hardback) |
ISBN 9781003053521 (ebook)
Subjects: LCSH: Customer relations. | Marketing.
Classification: LCC HF5415.5 .A436 2021 | DDC 658.8/12—dc23
LC record available at https://lccn.loc.gov/2020018619

ISBN: 978-0-367-47825-4 (hbk)
ISBN: 978-1-003-05352-1 (ebk)

Typeset in Times New Roman
by codeMantra

Contents

Figures

Tables

1 Introduction

Companies now are increasingly *"doing less product and service standardization and more niching and customization"* (Kotler and Keller, 2016:18). They understand their main goal in establishing a constructive dialogue with a customer, understanding his or her individual demands, and, based on this, offering the customer the product or service required (Kotler and Keller, 2016). This approach has formed the cornerstone of customer centricity (Fader and Toms, 2018). According to Pemberton (2018), customer centricity is a strategic priority for the most companies and *"the new marketing battlefront"*.

Tesco (2017:11), which is one of the leaders in retail industry, has claimed that, *"We place customers at the center of everything we do to deliver our purpose – serving shoppers a little better every day"*. Global clothing and sports goods manufacturer Adidas (2012:3) declared that *"we are consumer-focused"*. Samsung (2017:50), taking a lead in the production of consumer electronics and smartphones, has affirmed that, *"Customer satisfaction constitutes one of the most important fundamental factors in securing a company's competitive edge…"*.

Fader and Toms (2018) state that a constant focus on customers and consideration of their needs enables long-term financial value for the company. It is illustrated with the example of Procter & Gamble (2003:2), whose purpose is to improve the lives of their customers, stimulating them to provide *"leadership sales, profit and value creation, allowing the company's people, shareholders, and the communities in which company live and work to prosper"*. Adidas (2017:28) also argued that *"sharp focus on our consumers' need"* allowed the company to increase sales and financial performance.

The results of studies concerned with customer centricity illustrate that the higher the level of customer centricity, the greater the profit growth of the company (Vader, 2018). It is necessary to emphasize that customer centricity is not only about offering goods or services that meet customers' needs. As Burns (1978:465) has pointed out, transactional approach, when a company offers its customers a product or service, expecting their loyalty, is a *"superficial and trivial one"* and assumes just a *"short-lived relationship because sellers and buyers cannot repeat the identical exchange, both must move to the new level of gratification"*.

Studies reflect that having a long-term rather than a short-lived relationship with customers is more conducive for improving the company's revenue (Kumar, 1999). For example, in a financial sector, according to Reichheld (2001), a 5% increase in regular customers' share *"produces more than a 25% increase in profit"*.

The fundamental of long-term cooperation, according to Kotler and Keller (2016), rests on the trust between the customer and the company. Contemporary customers prefer to purchase products *"from companies they trust"* (Ernst & Young, 2013:3). When the customers are convinced that the company can be trusted, they begin to feel more confident. The company and the customer unite on the basis of such values as trust and transparency, seeing each other as partners. Trust-based relationships allow creating a low-risk trusting environment (Harvard Analytics Services, 2019). As Maslow (1970:6) posited, *"love of safety as it is of the love of truth"* are among the key basic human needs.

For example, Adidas (2017), Tesco (2018), and Samsung (2016) stressed that building trusting relationships with customers and partners is one of their top priorities. Paliszkiewicz and Klepacki (2013:1287) highlighted that, *"It's a proven fact that building customer trust in products, service and company is a great way to increase profits and build a strong, dependable consumer base"*.

Thus, building up a customer-centric company requires both offering a product or service that would meet the customer's needs and arranging a trusting, risk-free atmosphere of cooperation, leading to long-term relationships. According to the adaptive theory of leadership, these are complex tasks, when the company's leader is required to involve all employees, provide continuous training, and focus work of the entire company on innovative and non-standard solutions (Northouse, 2016). For example, achieving trust is a complex and ongoing process requiring very specific company's resources and competence of the personnel to continuously show transparency and integrity toward the customers (Consumer Policy Research Centre, 2017). Morgan (2018) observed that, *"Trust is the cornerstone to all customer experiences. It can't be built in a day, but it can be destroyed quickly"*.

The analysis of vacancies placed on designated recruitment websites like Indeed.com and Monster.com has indicated that companies show great interest for the experts who can arrange delivering of customer experience for the company. Fazackerley (no data), Director of Customer Experience at O2 mobile operator, has highlighted that customers are fundamental for any company's success.

According to Goasduff (2019), in a near-time perspective, the lack of customer centricity will lead to failure in 30% of business projects in the field of digital technologies. This is not surprising, because the contemporary customer is characterized by high expectations and a potential desire to terminate business relationships in the event of unsatisfactory experience from the contacts with the company (Panetta, 2017). As the Walker (2013) studies indicate, the customer will completely determine a company's activity, and companies will either have to take it for granted or leave the market.

Companies will simply have to become more customer-oriented, following the wants and expectations of customers. Ernst & Young (2013) has stated that companies, in their activities, will have to constantly look for the answer to a simple question, "What do customers want?" and build the policy based on their preferences. It is noted that such approach is *"a matter of survival"* (KPMG, 2017:4).

These facts illustrate that business will increasingly need a proven and clear marketing concept that explains the basic principles of forming an approach to creating an effective customer experience. In order to offer business a valuable and unambiguous solution to this issue, this study will identify and critically analyze the most effective marketing concept that allows a company to build productive and mutually beneficial interaction with customers. The relevance of this concept will be tested through the example of Amazon, which defines customer centricity as its main competitive advantage. Amazon CEO Jeff Bezos has clearly said that *"teams all across Amazon are listening to customers and wandering on their behalf!"* (Amazon, 2018:4).

2 Research Design

The research design of the study consists of the following sections.

Aim of the Study

To offer the best possible concept of forming a customer-centric company.

Study Objectives to Attain the Aim

1 Through the study of academic and business literature and documented information sources to analyze the marketing concepts of forming a customer-centric approach for business (marketing myopia, direct marketing, relationship marketing, and holistic marketing).
2 To choose the most effective marketing concept for the creation of a customer-centered company.
3 To conduct a detailed analysis of the most effective concept for its theoretical and empirical verification and possible adjustment.
4 To verify the findings obtained with the example of Amazon, a company that declares customer centricity as its main strategic priority.
5 Relying on study results, to offer a final solution that contributes to the formation of a customer-centric company.

Object of the Study

The object of the study will be marketing concepts, as well as Amazon, through which the effectiveness of the proposed approach to forming a customer-centric company will be tested.

Subject of the Study

Relevance and reliability of the suggested approach to forming a customer-centric company.

Hypothesis of the Study

The company's leader and employees are the main source for building and developing customer centricity.

Data Collection Techniques

- The study will rely on both qualitative parameters, involving the analysis of non-numeric data, and quantitative ones, including the analysis of various statistic data.
- *Literature review* and *document analysis* will be used as tools for collecting information.
  - *Literature review.* The purpose is to critically evaluate existing research to determine *"constructs potentially related to the phenomenon of interest"* and identify a knowledge gap (Bhattacherjee, 2012:21).
  - *Document analysis.* The purpose is a systematic procedure for checking or evaluating documents to gain new knowledge (Bowen, 2009).

Relevant academic and business literature will be used as information material for the analysis. Documentary sources of information will also be used: annual reports of companies, statistical databases, research reports, and so on.

The Main Value of the Research

- Customer-centered companies will get an opportunity of comparing their approach with the suggested concept and of determining the optimal variant for the further development of customer experience.
- Companies intending to develop customer centricity will get a comprehensible and verified concept of building customer experience.

Abbreviations

CX – Customer experience
CXM – Customer experience model

Analysis of the Notions

Certain notions presented in this study will undergo a detailed analysis with the purpose of defining their sense in a clear-cut way. Here belong such notions as *"customer experience"* and *"customer centricity"*.

Customer Experience

It is emphasized that the creation of a high-level customer experience is the strategic goal of the company's management (Lemon and Verhoev, 2016). Such close attention to this notion is caused by the fact that a positive link was observed between the customer experience and the company's successful financial outcomes (Hernandez, 2016). According to the results of study, 86% of buyers would pay more for the better customer experience (Walker in Kulbyte, 2016).

Lemon and Verhoev (2016) remark that CX is the experience obtained by a customer by means of communicating with the company, and this experience may prompt and encourage him or her to pursue further cooperation with the company, as well as on the contrary, impel to stop cooperation.

Consequently, the company must make every effort to make the process of cooperation with it valuable for the client and produce only a positive impression upon him or her to facilitate further cooperation. Giménez (2018) emphasizes that a customer is ready to cooperate with a company only if its suggestion proves to be really valuable. It is noted that the company should engineer and develop its unique experience encouraging a customer to cooperation (Lemon and Verhoev, 2016). However, while creating this experience, the company must be expressly guided by the voice of the customer, by his or her requirements, the realization of which will have a positive impact on the customer's desire to cooperate with the company (Fritz, 2018).

The company will always be able to improve customer experience, on the basis of its existed experience, its bulk of knowledge, and using Lewinian's experiential learning cycle (Kolb, 1984). This cycle shows clearly which stages should be passed to create new knowledge and approaches to solving issues on the basis of the experience obtained (Figure 2.1).

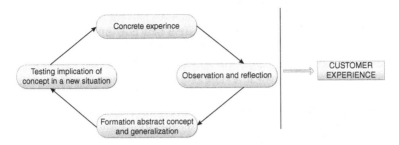

Figure 2.1 The application of Lewinian's experiential learning cycle for the improvement of customer experience.

In respect to *customer experience*, the components of the cycle can be interpreted in the following way:

- *"Concrete experience"* is the company's customer experience which it proposes to a customer.
- *"Observation and reflection"* is the evaluation of the customer experience obtained and realized, the analysis of existing approaches to creating and developing it.
- *"Formation of abstract concept and generalization"* is the improvement, change, or creation of the radically new customer experience.
- *"Testing the implication of concept in a new situation"* is the testing of obtained results in practice.

It is necessary to note that the given cycle can start with any stage (Bassot, 2016).

For instance, if a company lacks its own experience, it can start with the *observation and reflection* of the existing approaches to creating *customer experience*. The main aim is their conceptualization, comprehension, and transformation into practical actions for creating its unique CX. The creation of *customer experience*, on the basis of the analysis of one's own experience, with the use of Lewinian's experiential learning cycle allows:

1 To determine what was useful from the previous experience can be applied in the future.
2 To determine which company's actions managed or failed to create values for customers.

3   To define areas requiring further improvement or a complete change.
4   To adjust the existing or to create a new customer experience, which is valuable for the client.

Therefore, a company is in a state of continuous learning and, consequently, of developing the CX. This facilitates its continual improvement and the creation of value necessary for the customer.

It is also necessary to note that concentrating only on its own experience, without conducting benchmarking, the company reduces its possibilities in CX creation. According to Boxwell (1994), benchmarking provides an opportunity of analyzing external standards and learning from other experience, which allows to upgrade the existing practice.

So, CX is allowing a company to create the value necessary for the customer and to improve mutual interaction by means of continuing analysis and the development of knowledge obtained, skills, and experience.

Customer Centricity

Customer centricity is the concept of company development, which implicates focusing exclusively on meeting customers' requirements by means of creating and realization of positive customer experience (Hollader et al., 2013; Shah et al., 2006).

To realize *customer centricity* and, as a consequence, to create a positive CX, the following requirements must be fulfilled in a company (Blanchard, 2007; Fader and Toms, 2018; Weinstein and Hank, 2012):

- Presence of the vision of the company development and of values underlining the importance of customer centricity.
- Structuring of all company processes around the customer's interests.
- Customer-centered personnel and culture.
- Continuing bilateral cooperation with the customer.
- Providing the customer with the product/service fully meeting his or her requirements.
- Evaluation of the CX suggested to the customer and its constant development.

So, *customer centricity* and *customer experience* are interconnected notions:

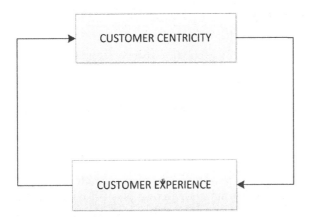

Figure 2.2 Interconnection between "*customer centricity*" and "*customer experience*".

- *Customer centricity* is the concept of the company development, based on meeting the client's needs and requirements.
- *Customer experience* is the result of compliance with these requirements, which is expressed in cooperation with the customers and creation of value required by them.

By following the requirements of customer-centered approach, the company enlarges the share of its loyal clients, which produces a positive impact on its revenue (Kelly, 2018; Shah et al., 2006).

3 Analysis of the Marketing Concepts

For the purpose of accomplishing the research objectives of this book, the following marketing concepts will be analyzed in this chapter: "marketing myopia", "direct marketing", "relationship marketing", and "holistic marketing". On the basis of the conducted analysis, the most effective marketing concept for the further detailed analysis will be determined.

"Marketing Myopia" by Theodore Levitt

In 1960 Theodore Levitt suggested a marketing concept implying focus not on a manufactured product, which is a groundless myopia, but on customers' requirements. Levitt noted that *"An industry begins with the customer and his needs, not with a patent, a raw material, or a selling skill"* (Levitt, 1960:55). As one of the examples, Detroit automobile industry was considered, which, in Levitt's (1960:51) opinion, was *"mainly product-oriented, not customer-oriented"*. It was empathized that automobile companies did not pay enough attention to after-sales services, and this was inconvenient for the customers. According to Levitt (1960), only 57 out of 7000 Chevrolet dealers provided the highly sought night service. This fact showed clearly that the companies demonstrated marketing myopia, focusing exclusively on the product and not concentrating on the customer's desires and needs. A research in 2014 showed that seven out of ten customers prefer buying the goods from the companies providing a better service (Joabar in American Express, 2017).

Levitt (1960) underlined that before introducing a new automobile, it is necessary to ask a customer what kind of an auto he or she wants to have. It is an *"illusion that a superior product will sell itself"* (Levitt, 1960:54).

Against this general background of studies on product centricity, Lee Iacocca stood out, who worked in the Ford Corporation between 1946 and 1978 and rose through the ranks from an engineer to become the president of Ford Motor Company (*Encyclopedia Britannica*, 2019). Abodaher (1985:159) states that one of the reasons of Lee Iacocca's success as CEO of Ford was his desire to *"find out what kind of car Americans wanted"*. Levitt's theoretical insights, proclaiming that a company should be governed by customers' requirements, found their support with practical actions as far back as then.

So, according to Levitt (1960), customer centricity is the mandatory consideration of customers' requirements and desires in the process of a product's creation. It is necessary to note that marketing myopia is based on the transactional approach, when a customer, buying a product or a service meeting his or her requirements, demonstrated his or her loyalty to a brand. As it was already mentioned, in Burns' (1978) opinion, such approach doesn't result in creating stable long-term links between a company and its clients.

"Direct Marketing" by Lester Wunderman

In 1967, Wunderman developed the concept of *direct marketing* (Sexton, 2013). Similar to Levitt, Wunderman keeps the main stress on the idea that a customer is an initial point for any business.

But Wunderman's (1998) suggestion is the personification of the contacts with a customer by creating individual relationships with him or her, fostering with this the customer's loyalty to the brand. A vivid example of direct marketing is demonstrated by Facebook, offering to its users the decisions coinciding with their Internet requirements in the shape of an individual advertisement Internet message.

Direct marketing is considered by Wunderman as a new company strategy targeted at the creation of stable individual client links. Wunderman (1967 in lesterwunderman.com, 2014) emphasized that *"We are living in an age of re-personalization. People, product and services are all seeking an individual identity"*. According to Subramanian (2017), today the absence of direct contacts with the customer can have a very negative impact on his or her further motivation to offer cooperation with the company, and, as a consequence, on incremental volumes of sales.

The key role in the personalization of each customer's requirements, according to Wunderman (1967 in lesterwunderman.com, 2014), will be played by computer technologies, with the help of which it will be possible to remember and analyze individual customer preferences and *"link these facts to advertising and selling must evolve—where advertising and buying become a single action"*. Kottler and Keller (2016) note that at present marketing professionals must be sure of their knowledge of their clients' preferences and they should personalize their suggestions accordingly.

In sum, according to direct marketing concept, customer centricity is the company's ability to hear *"the voice of the customer"* with the purpose of meeting his or her individual preferences. This is the basic difference of the described concept from *"marketing myopia"*, in which only the customers' collective opinion is considered, with a view to mass production. The given approach is a shift away from transactional relations: simply goods in exchange of loyalty; it has the best possible effect on the creation of long-term relations between the company and its customers.

"Relationship Marketing" by Leonard Berry

In 1983 Berry introduced the concept of *"relationship marketing"* (Berry, 1995). The main point of the concept is that the emphasis must be placed first of all on retention and broadening bonds with the already existing customers (Berry, 1995). One of the issues defining the necessity of customer retention is the fact that a company spends 5 to 25 times more money on winning new customers than on the retention of already existing ones (Gallo, 2014). Moreover, according to a 2018 study, it is getting harder and harder for companies to invite new customers (Redbord, 2018). The main reason of this phenomenon is customers' distrust of businesses; consequently, companies will have to put in an enormous effort to win the confidence of new customers (Redbord, 2018).

At the same time, Reichheld (2001) gives some data from research, quoting that, for instance, in the financial sector *"return customers tend to buy more from a company over time"*. In hotel business, customer retention also produces a positive influence on the profit of the business (Khan, 2013). These facts and figures testify to the strategic importance of existing customers' retention and of building long-term relations with them.

Berry notes that relationship marketing is especially important for service companies. According to Ramamoorthy (2000), service industry embraces companies, the activity of which lies in satisfaction of people's compelling needs. The most typical examples are banks, insurance companies, tourist agencies, repair services, and so on. The necessity of such companies applying relationship marketing is determined by the fact that they have an acute need for repeat purchases made by already existing customers. Bain observes that an average regular customer spends 67% more during the 31–36 months of his relations with business than during the 0–6 months (Bain & Company, 1999 in Baveja et al., no data).

Meanwhile, beyond the service industry, the trend of customer retention is observed. Johnson et al. (1997:142) note that the companies in automobile industry have been paying attention not only to the product quality but also to *"customer loyalty and retention"* for quite some time now. Such an industrial giant as General Electric also pays attention to building long-term relations with its customers. It is stated that successful financial results of the GE Digital department are largely obtained due to *"significant improvements in retention and customer satisfaction"* (Kocher, no data). Thus, relationship marketing is a cross-industrial instrument providing the creation of a customer-centered approach.

Grönroos and Helle (2010) observe that in sum each business is service oriented. And indeed, a company must not only create a product but provide its service, creating a top-value proposition for the customer.

According to Berry (1995), there exist three levels of creating a value on the basis of which long-term customer relations are built:

1 *Financial level*: providing goods or services at prices that are affordable for the customers and are usually lower than competitors' prices. This approach has a low effectiveness rate, as it is easily copied by competitors. A vivid example is low-cost airlines, which desire to expand their competitive advantages considerably not only due to price leadership (Saeed, 2016). Ryanair, for instance, is a powerful brand, which is quite trustworthy with its customers (Saeed, 2016). The low-cost carrier "Berlin Air" won its position as the best low-cost airline by proposing to its customers an exceptional service. This achievement became possible due to the company's own effective program of personnel training (Saeed, 2016).

2 *Social level*, which means a constant bilateral communication with customers. Adidas (2018) has created and continues expanding its unique *"digital ecosystem"* numbering over 500 million users with whom the company maintains contact by means of various digital communication channels. It is necessary to note that the members of this *"digital ecosystem"* are also the

most probable buyers of the company's products. Adidas (2018) states that it intends enlarging its investments in building links with the company's customers for deeper understanding of their requirements.

Berry (1995:242) emphasizes that *"communications must be open, honest, and frequent"*. It is noted that it is these regular communications through which a company offers information, which is interesting for its customers, that facilitate the establishment of long-term relations (*Forbes*, 2013).

So, a *"social level"* has a higher value as the continuous interaction with the company facilitates the establishment of social relationship between the company and the customer and the upgrading of loyalty level (Berry, 1995). To create similar social relationships, competitors will have to invest quite a lot of efforts. So, according to Shah et al. (2006:116), *"customer loyalty is the key to long-run profitability"*.

Due to mutual communications, customers will also have a more indulgent attitude to possible service failures, and the company will have time to remedy the current problems quickly and effectively (Berry, 1995).

3   *Structural level* is the company's proposition of a unique solution of the customers' problems by providing a quality service (product). It has a very high effectiveness rate as the customers can see that the company is offering a service or a product that can meet their needs. For instance, Tesla offers its customers, who bought its automobile, installation of a special application due to which they can swiftly register their maintenance service or rework. Besides, Tesla states that its *"service team is available 24/7, 365 days a year"* (Tesla, no data). In this context, Deloitte (2014:7) stresses that *"The majority of customers do not want amazing service, instead they want clear and accurate information on the service they will receive"*.

Thus, the structural level enables the companies to offer a unique proposition based upon the product or service quality and additional benefits facilitating full satisfaction of the customer's needs.

The highest value for a customer is the simultaneous use of financial, social, and structural levels: a reasonable price, the relevant value of the product or a service, which facilitates the solution of the customer's problems, and the establishment of bilateral communications of the "company–customer" type (Berry, 1995).

A special stress is made by Berry (1995) on the fact that a service must be a quality one. Stevenson (2015) stresses that a dissatisfactory quality of a product or service will not facilitate customer retention and will do a considerable harm to a company's image and reputation.

Besides, the creation of a unique customer proposition, according to Berry (1995:241), will be facilitated by internal marketing, the essence of which is that the company is *"attracting, motivating, developing and retaining qualified employees"*.

It is specifically due to the company's personnel, according to Berry, that customer cooperation is accomplished. In other words, customer centricity is the result of the cooperation of an internal stakeholder (the personnel) with an external stakeholder (the customers). Thus, by developing the personnel's adherence to a customer-centered strategy and its ability to provide the necessary competent support, the company will considerably improve its relations with the customers. It is noted that the longer the personnel works in the company, the greater is its readiness to demonstrate the highest customer centricity degree, because *"long-term employees know more about the business and have had more opportunity to develop bonds"* (Berry, 1995:241).

Within the relationship marketing concept, attention is paid to the fact that for successful development of relationships with customers, the company needs the cooperation with *"noncustomer groups"* consisting of external stakeholders (Berry, 1995:242). Here belong about 30 stakeholders, among them there are investors, suppliers, mass media, and government (Gummesson, 1994 in Berry, 1995). It is assumed that the company will consider independently which particular stakeholders exert a strategic impact on the customer cooperation level and which of them will establish productive relationships with customers based on full confidence (Berry, 1995).

As an example, the company's relations with its strategic partner, that is, suppliers, should be considered. It so widely known that in many companies manufacturing of end product or service is closely connected with a strong collaboration with suppliers providing necessary components or service. For instance, Samsung emphasizes that the relationships with key partners, suppliers, are strategic ones and are based on the philosophy of fairness, openness, and partner cooperation (Samsung, 2018). It is stated in General Electric (2018) that the quality of their work with suppliers determines such important indices of the company effectiveness as operating costs and their products' competitive performance.

Within the relationship marketing concept, like in direct marketing, the emphasis is placed on the necessity of considering customers' individual requirements. Besides, Berry stresses the importance of offering exceptional service and attention to customers who generate top value for the company.

The emphasis is made on the issue that the main condition of successful relationship marketing is that it must be *"built on the foundation of trust"* (Berry, 1995:242). For instance, if the quality declared by the company is not in compliance with the real product quality, it will have a negative impact on a buying desire (Saleem et. al, 2015). Relations based on trust reduce uncertainty in the interaction between customers and the company, making them long term and more stable.

Thus, customer centricity, according to Berry, is a complex phenomenon aimed at providing value to the company's customers for maintaining and enhancing relationships. Value for customers is formed by simultaneous application of three levels of relationship marketing – financial, social, and structural. Berry especially underlines the key role of the company personnel and the necessity of cooperation with the company's stakeholders from "noncustomer groups", which positively effects the development of customer centricity.

It is necessary to note that relationship marketing is a complete and final withdrawal from transactional relations of the product or service in exchange for customer loyalty. By offering customers long-term relationship, based on trust and openness, and by considering individual wishes, the company makes maximum effort to satisfy them. Such an approach fully facilitates the realization of the principle that customers always come *"first"* and then the profit (McKinsey & Company, 2017).

"Holistic Marketing" by Philipp Kotler and Kevin Lane Keller

In early 2000s, a new concept called *"holistic marketing"* was introduced by Kotler and Keller (2006). Its main idea is that all company's functions and marketing activities must be interrelated. According to Kotler and Keller (2016), due to interrelated work of all departments, a company can create the most effective cooperation strategy with customers and other stakeholders, which will produce a positive impact on its development and profit. For instance, on the basis of customer needs determined by the marketing department, the company engineers develop products, financiers invest the necessary funding, suppliers purchase respective materials, and the production services manufacture the required products. It is due to such an approach that the company will be able to create a real valuable proposition to the customers.

Kotler and Keller (2002) emphasize that customer centricity presupposes the responsibility of all the company's departments. By way of illustration, Xerox Company is introduced; it is stated in each employee's job description how this or that position can influence the development of customer centricity (Kotler and Keller, 2002).

Actually, holistic marketing consists of four interrelated equally weighted elements (Figure 3.1):

- Relationship marketing
- Integrated marketing
- Internal marketing
- Performance marketing

Figure 3.1 The holistic marketing concept.

To determine each element's contribution to the development of a company's marketing activity, they will be considered in depth.

Relationship Marketing

The main target of relationship marketing is the creation of stable relations with stakeholders, who directly or indirectly influence the company's work, with the aim of profit generation and business development (Kotler and Keller, 2016). It is pointed out that the company must build relations with the following stakeholders: *"customers, employees, marketing partners (channels, suppliers, distributors, dealers, agencies), and members of the financial community (shareholders, investors, analysts)"* (Kotler and Keller, 2016:43). It is emphasized that the company should generate value for all the stakeholders. For instance, the cooperation with such a stakeholder as supplier will finally help in delivering value to customers. Procter & Gamble (no data) clearly declare that together with suppliers, they *"work together to bring great products to life for consumers around the world"*. Adidas (2018), understanding the importance of shareholders, in their annual report, dedicates a special chapter, which tells in detail what the company achieved during the reporting period, how it intends to develop, and how it plans to pay dividends. According to Carrol and Buchholtz (2009), shareholders can have a considerable impact on the company's strategy; consequently, their requirements must be appreciated on a mandatory basis. Besides, Adidas (2018) emphasizes that the company welfare is in direct proportion to the welfare of all its stakeholders – consumers, athletes, teams, partners, and shareholders.

Further, Kotler and Keller (2016) determine customers to be the most important stakeholders, because the company's profit and its successful development depend on the level of cooperation with them. To create stronger customer bonds, the company should formulate individual propositions to its customers, following on from their former purchase experience and preferences. Besides, it is emphasized that a company should pay special attention to customers who generate the biggest financial value for it by introducing special cooperation conditions for them.

Kotler and Keller (2016) draw special attention to the need of the company's cooperation with society and communities. It is stated that people will more willingly buy the product of the company that demonstrates its care for society and for the environment.

The stress is also made on the fact that mutually beneficial partnership both with customers, and with all other stakeholders, grounded on transparency and trust, will allow a company to create its unique marketing network. For instance, many companies sell their products by means of third-party distributors. After uniting them into its marketing network and building mutually beneficial relationships with them, a company will doubtlessly get a competitive advantage, in the form of reliable marketing channels.

According to Kotler and Keller (2016:80), *"Companies no longer compete – marketing networks do"*, exercising the most positive impact on the company's profit. However, it is necessary to note that *"If maximizing profit is the ultimate goal, a company will not prosper in the long run"* (Verhage, 2013:20).

A vivid illustrative example to this statement is Ranbaxy, an Indian pharmaceutical company. Its vision for the greatest sales market, the United States, was that its earnings at this market should be $1 billion (Eban, 2019). But, as it was proved in practice, the company realized its vision through the falsification of clinical research results, which enabled shortening the terms of a preparation's entry into the market (Eban, 2019). As a consequence, medicines with unsubstantiated effectiveness got into the market. This meant that the health of these products' consumers was set at stake. In 2013, after a thorough investigation exercised by American authorities, the biggest generic drug maker Ranbaxy Laboratories Ltd. pleaded guilty to security violation while manufacturing medicinal products and agreed to pay a fine of $500 million (Reuters, 2013). Moreover, the company was constantly accused of conducting business contrary to ethical standards (Reuters, 2013). Ranbaxy no longer exists today. It was acquired by the pharmaceutical company Sun Pharmaceutical Industries Ltd, with due regard for *"betting it can fix factory quality glitches that plagued the current owner"* (Kim and Siddiqui, 2014).

Therefore, it should be stressed again that companies should follow the principle that their target in building marketing networks is a mutually rewarding, confidence-based cooperation with customers and key stakeholders. This approach will ensure the company's necessary profit and development.

Integrated Marketing

According to Kotler and Keller (2016:44), integrated marketing is grounded on the idea that *"the whole is greater than the sum of its parts"*. This postulate is the reflection of holism principles, which state that a whole is the result of interconnection of its parts (Jackson, 2003). Guided by this principle, Kotler and Keller (2016) state that the most effective value proposition can be notified to a customer if all information channels are integrated and constitute a complete whole. An example of integrated marketing communications can be seen in the specifics of conducting advertisement events of GoPro Company, which produces video cameras. Their pages in social networks are united with one appeal: *"We make the world's most versatile camera"* (Twitter, YouTube, TripAdvisor, no data). The company, using various promotional videos and photos and a unique slogan, demonstrates that its cameras are all-purpose ones and they can be used in any, even most extreme, conditions. This condition is critically important for GoPro company's potential customers.

Internal Marketing

This element is directly related to the company's personnel. The thrust is placed on the fact that the personnel must fully share the policy of customer centricity. With this aim, a company provides for *"hiring, training, and motivating able employees who want to serve customers well"* (Kotler and Keller, 2016:45).

Kotler and Keller (2016:45) emphasize that there is no *"sense to promise excellent service before the company's staff is ready to provide it"* (Kotler and Keller, 2016). It is underlined that the biggest effect in creating a top-value proposition for a customer is achieved by means of the approach when the work in all departments is interconnected (Kotler and Keller, 2016). Adidas (2018:144) remarks that their brand's strength is generated from the interconnection of the following actions: launch of new innovative products to the market, *"inspiring marketing campaign"* and *"successful execution of the company strategic business plan"*. Therefore, to maintain their brand's strength, Adidas places their stress on the need for interconnected work of production departments, marketing, and other actions, stated in their strategic development plan.

In Kotler's (2002) view, the collaborative work of all departments must be supported by the realization of the company's vision, which defines the customer as the key strategic priority. Thus, any company's decision will be taken with a consideration of customer's interests, which will certainly produce a positive impact on the development of customer experience.

It is stressed specially that the effectiveness of internal marketing, and consequently, customer centricity depends on the respective behavior demonstrated by the company's top management, who set an example for other company employees (Kotler and Keller, 2016).

In sum, within internal marketing framework, the existence of a direct link is underlined between the level of the personnel development, its devotion to the customer-centered approach, and the company's ability to create effective CX for its customers.

Performance Marketing

The main task of performance marketing is the evaluation of the effectiveness of the company's marketing activity and its influence on business success (Kotler and Keller, 2016). Kotler and Keller (2016:18, 47) note that companies should move beyond financial indices, evaluating not only *"customer loss rate, customer satisfaction, product quality..."*

but such indices as *"legal, ethical, social, and environmental effects of marketing activities and programs"* on customers, other stakeholders, including the society. It is necessary to understand to which extent stakeholders are satisfied with cooperation, if the company generates necessary value for them, and how it is perceived in society. For instance, according to research, 92% will be more likely to trust a company that supports social or environmental issues (Butler, 2018). Therefore, measuring the level of trust of its customers, analyzing its influence on society, as well as ecology, the company will be able to predict the trend of financial change indices. This example demonstrates clearly the strategic importance of performance marketing, which allows the evaluation of the effectiveness of marketing activity, on the grounds of indices related to customer satisfaction rate as well as on the analysis of the company's influence on its key stakeholders, by means of evaluating legal, social, ethical, and other factors.

Conclusions

In summary, the analysis in this chapter showed that holistic marketing elements are closely connected with the company's cooperation with its customers and stakeholders:

1 Relationship marketing facilitates the creation of stable long-term bonds with the customers and other company's stakeholders.
2 Integrated marketing provides the interconnection of communication channels, facilitating the creation of the best value proposition for the customers.
3 Internal marketing is aimed at the development of a customer-centered approach among the personnel, due to which customer value is created.
4 Performance marketing determines the effectiveness of the company's marketing activity, the customer and stakeholder satisfaction rate, and the influence of these indices on the company's development.

Besides, holistic marketing has the following advantages over the concepts considered above:

1 Holistic marketing is the complex of four elements, performing different tasks. Veber (1964) stated that all tasks within an organization must be divided according to their functions. Such an

approach facilitates the further productive development of the organization due to the fact that concentration of employees on certain tasks brings forward more effective achievement of the result needed (Veber, 1964). Holistic marketing solves the task of the realization of customer-centered approach by means of dividing the elements according to their tasks: the creation of customer bonds, the development of the staff's customer-centered skills, the development of integrated communication channels, as well as the measurement of the success of exercised activities.

2   Kotler and Keller (2016) emphasize that all elements within the holistic marketing framework must be interrelated.

This approach solves the basic management problem which lies in the following: business is often considered rather as separate parts than as an interrelated summation of elements (Jackson, 2003). As an example, digitalization of CX should be considered; without the staff's serious training and their ability to work with new technologies, this innovation will not produce any positive impact on the CX effectiveness.

In other words, following the principle of elements' interrelation in the company, in the process of transition to digital channels of communication with the customers, the company must take care of the necessary training of the staff. As it was already stressed, in holistic marketing the main emphasis is placed on the issue of the interrelation of all elements so that they form an integrated whole.

3   Holistic marketing focuses attention on the importance of not merely cooperation of a company with its stakeholders but on generating value for them. This idea completely correlates with the provision of the stakeholder theory, which states that only in the case of mutually beneficial cooperation and generating value for its stakeholders a company can rely on their support, and consequently, on the achievement of desirable results (Freeman and Velamuri, 2005).

4   Holistic marketing pays attention to the fact that the success of company's marketing activities must be necessarily measured. Drucker (1986) stated that the measurement of the achieved results allows realizing the necessary control level, for changing and improving the processes.

It has been observed that holistic marketing elements are given close attention in the literature on the issues of customer centricity (Table 3.1).

Table 3.1 Presence of holistic marketing elements in literary sources on customer centricity

Relationship marketing	1	Senior managers must pay close attention to customer retention and to building long-term bonds with them (Mann, 2014).
	2	Relationship marketing has a strategic importance and produces a considerable influence on business' long-term success (Smith and Zook, 2011).
	3	The success of a contemporary company depends on the effectiveness rate of its cooperation with both internal and external stakeholders (Freeman and Dmitriev, 2017).
	4	Customer orientation and "total customer care" are key factors in global competition (Brännback, 1999).
Integrated marketing	1	All marketing communications must be integrated for the most complete CX achievement (Smith and Zook, 2011).
	2	The application of integrated marketing communications with the company's customers will allow the rise in sales and the company's profit (Pikton and Broderik, 2005).
	3	Integrated marketing communications play the most important role in the formation and development of the company's identity (Percy, 2014).
	4	Integrated marketing communications, grounded on holistic principles, are a unique tool, the application of which facilitates the establishment of long-term bonds with customers (Persuit and McDowell Marinchak, 2016).
Internal marketing	1	It is important that each employee had a clear idea of what customer centricity is and how it is realized in practice (Brännback, 1999).
	2	Only owing to its personnel the company will be able to understand its customer and form for him the top-value proposition (Hill, 2012).
	3	Top management must demonstrate their commitment to the customer-centered approach by setting a personal example (Mann, 2014).
	4	Customer centricity is the collective responsibility of the organization's personnel (Zafer, 2015).
Performance marketing	1	The measurement of marketing activity effectiveness is critically important as it allows to "understand what's working and what's broken" (Schmidt-Subramanian et al., 2016).
	2	The company's management must analyze the data related to the customer centricity rate, to answer the question if the company really generates customer value (Fader and Toms, 2018).
	3	Companies need to know how they are anticipated by the society, as the success of customer centricity depends of such knowledge (Reputation Institute, 2017).
	4	The measurement of realization of the success of customer centricity is a continuous process (GFK, 2017).

The holistic marketing concept is the optimal one to be considered further on as the model for creating a customer-centered company and value for the customers. Thus, customer centricity on the basis of application of holistic marketing is a complex process. As the result of interconnection of relationship marketing, integrated marketing, internal marketing, and performance marketing, and of interrelated work of all departments and communications, a value proposition for customers and key stakeholders is formed; marketing networks are created, allowing the company to develop successfully and to generate profit.

It is necessary to observe that the elements that holistic marketing consists of were worked out much earlier than the given concept. The term *"relationship marketing"* and the developed concept were introduced by Berry as early as in 1983 (Berry, 1995).

The importance of a company's personnel for a successful implementation of its marketing activity was highlighted by Sassen and Arbeit in 1976 (Sassen and Arbeit, 1976). The term *"internal marketing"* was introduced by George in 1977 and used by Berry in the relationship marketing concept (Berry, 1995). The creation of the term *"integrated marketing communications"* must be attributed to Schultz and goes back to the early 1990s (Shultz et al., 1993; Shultz and Kitchen, 1997).

The necessity of measuring processes in business, which obviously formed the foundation of performance marketing, was described by Drucker in 1986 (Drucker, 1986).Within the holistic marketing concept, this fact was united with the stakeholder theory provisions, which focuses on the company's direct influence on its stakeholders; therefore, the rate of such influence is to be measured. Measuring of the company's influence on the stakeholders is necessary, as in the event that the stakeholders are not satisfied with the cooperation, the company will find it difficult to <u>achieve</u> long-term stable development.

Besides, in holistic marketing the postulates of the analyzed concepts are used, namely, *"marketing myopia,"* which means the necessity of hearing the customer's voice and *"direct marketing"* related to creating individual bonds with customers.

It also should be noted that the necessity of holistic approach to the creation of customer value proposition of the top rank was also observed earlier by Berry within the framework of the relationship marketing concept (1993). Berry emphasized that the best result is achieved by simultaneous application of financial, social, and structural levels, which means fixing of a logical price, the service (product) meeting the customer's requirements, and effective bilateral communications (Berry, 1995).

All these facts again underline holistic marketing's greatest relevance for a more detailed analysis of its application in the process of creating a customer-centered company and CX development, as it considers reliable, previously verified concepts and their key points.

4 Holistic Marketing as the Basis of Effective Customer Experience Creation

The analysis done thus far shows that there exist grounds for a more thorough study of holistic marketing, as it presents an optimal concept that can be practically applied in the process of creating a customer-centered company. Thus, in this chapter, holistic marketing elements will be given a more detailed consideration, the purpose being their best adaptation for the creation of a customer-centered company.

According to Gartner (2018), nearly 50% of organizations, participating in the survey, stated that customer centricity had a positive influence on their financial indexation. Moreover, 80% of the organizations consider that it is on the level of customer centricity that the main competition among companies is going to take place (Gartner, 2018).

So, customer centricity is considered by companies to be not only an important strategic advantage but also a condition for a successful development and continuation on the market. However, the question arises: where does the creation of a customer-centered company and the customer experience formation start?

Internal Marketing

Subramanian (2018) emphasizes that the process of creating a customer-centered company *"starts with their employees"*. According to Clarke and Kinghorn (2018), personnel's incompetence, their inability to cooperate with customers, as well as the low-quality service and lack of confidence are stated as basic reasons impelling a customer to break relations with the company.

Verhage (2013:23) notes that *"all employees –including the receptionist and cashiers – have to be well-trained and motivated to satisfy the customers"*. Macgillavry and Synian (2016) place emphasis on the fact that customer centricity rate is directly related to the degree of how much this approach is shared by all the company's personnel. Samsung (2017) states that people are a key factor of its success. Adidas (2018), realizing the importance of people in the company, annually works out the *"people strategy"*, which is a part of their general strategy. Thus, the key role of personnel in customer centricity development, as well as in company's business development, is recognized both academically and practically.

Consequently, internal marketing, an element of holistic marketing element and aimed at the development of the employees' customer-centered approach, can be considered as the foundation for customer centricity. Hill (2012) observes that due to its personnel, a company will be able to offer the best CX to its customers.

In this context, Fader and Toms (2018) note that the most important condition of creating a customer-centered company is leadership. Burns (2003) remarks that leadership and the leader are inseparable notions. Welch (2005:85) puts an emphasis on the fact that the leader, possessing *"deep knowledge"* and *"strong persuasion skills"*, gives energy to other employees. Senge (2004) focuses on the fact that the leader's behavior easily morphs into general norms and rules in the company. The leader can both break an old behavior model and suggest a new one (Senge, 2004). According to Bass (1990), it is the leader who plays the key role in the transformation of people's consciousness, facilitating that by a complete change in the organization's essentiality.

So, the leader sets an example for the employees and is the protagonist of the company's transformation. Consequently, the leader will be the main protagonist, the "starting point" in the process of the creation of a customer-centered company.

However, Burns (2003) stresses that leadership cannot be considered without the leader's cooperation with the followers, and that leadership is a collective phenomenon. Hiller and Beauchesne (2014) observe that top management also *"influences individuals and teams"*. Therefore, the leader, in cooperation with the top management that adopts the customer centricity policy, will be able to facilitate the spreading of this approach in the company more effectively. As a result, employees in their work get driven by the idea that observation of the customer's interests is a priority. Carlyle (1840) stated that the leader is a figure to follow.

According to Peppers and Rogers (2011), the transformation of a company into a customer-centered one requires, alongside with leadership, the relevant vision, which determines the customer to be the main strategic priority. According to Welch (2005), the key role in determining the vision of the company's development belongs to the leader. Bennis (2003) points out that the leader must demonstrate through personal example the vision's realization and be dedicated to this vision. It is also pointed out that in his actions the leader must give consideration to customer's point of view, whilst observing the interests of the company's key stakeholders – employees, customers, and society (Bennis, 2003).

An example of the leader's vision, in the way the company should organize its relations with the customers and other stakeholders, is demonstrated by Tony Hsieh, CEO of Zappos, the online shoe and clothing retailer. In his letter to the employees, Hsieh (2009) states that *"our vision remains the same: delivering happiness to customers, employees, and vendors. We just want to get there faster"*.

Hsieh (2009) also pointed the definite steps that will allow making Zappos' customer and stakeholders happier: *"developing relationships, creating personal emotional connections, and delivering high touch ("WOW") customer service"*. It is necessary to note that Zappos is one of the top customer-centered companies in the world (Morgan, 2018).

It was emphasized that 78% of the staff in companies with effective CX state their full understanding of customer-centered vision and the company's development (Yohn, 2018). This fact provides another demonstration of the vision's strategic role in the process of creating a customer-centered company.

An important role in the realization of the customer-centered vision is played by the employees' commitment to values. Whitley (2006) writes that values determine the very essence of the company, making it unique and different from other companies. For instance, the first Zappos' value is worded as follows: *"Deliver WOW through Service"* (Zappos, no data). It determines the essence of the service company, to which Zappos belongs, helps in the realization of the company's vision, and gives a clear-cut signal of the principle that providing exclusive service to the customer is a key duty of the company's employees.

However, Whitley (2006) highlights the idea that it is impossible to persuade people in somebody's version of the reality, because nothing is the reality for them unless they take part in its creation. Blanchard (2007) focuses on the fact that leadership is not done for people, it is done with people.

Thus, the leader and the company's top management must invite the participation of all employees in the creation and development of CX. The conditions must be created in the company to ensure that all employees participate in this process. For instance, this can be achieved with the help of a procedure asking each employee to submit his or her suggestions for creating and developing customer experience. In Zappos (no data), it is stated that they encourage their employees *"to identify areas of opportunity within the organization and propose solutions"*.

Besides, the most important task is fixing the limit of leadership. Tisch (cited in Field, 2008) remarks that *"senior management cannot be in the field all the time"*. Fixing the leadership limit is facilitated by delegating of powers related to the creation of customer centricity to the employees. However, this possibility is conditioned by the provision of continuous development of customer centricity skills (Brännback, 1999). The personnel, in Brännback's (1999) opinion, must know *"how to provide a solution to the needs of the customer"*. That is why the company, in addition to demonstration of the employees' personal dedication to customer centricity, must provide for the development of corresponding skills and values for all categories of personnel without exception. It is stated that a modern company in the post-industrial society requires a quick reaction, sometimes anticipating the situation, and this is possible only if learning and development take place on a continuous basis (de Geus, 1998).

The development of personnel's customer centricity can be accomplished by using the following methods (Markey and Reichheld, 2013):

- Training employees on customer centricity development and implementation of the company's values, linked with CX, into real practice.
- High-velocity feedback. It allows reinforcing the knowledge obtained at the training by analyzing the customers' feedback. The employee can see whether his or her actions for the customer were effective.
- Observation and coaching. Although a customer's feedback allows to understand where improvements are required, the participation of a "coach or skilled observer" will help the employees to see more tellingly what must be changed in their interrelations with the customers, and in what way.

Besides, the creation of communities of practice (CoP) in the company is rather useful. These are employee groups united by professional interests and the desire to develop their professional skills on a continuous basis (Wenger, 1998).

With the help of CoP, where the employees would share their experience of customer centricity and communicate with corresponding experts, the company would facilitate the improvement of professionalism and spread of necessary knowledge (Wenger-Trayner and Wenger-Trayner, 2015). As Wenger observes, CoP participants bear collective responsibility for governing and spreading of knowledge (Wenger, 2006).

Intensive attention to employee development leads to the creation of *"learning organizations" "where people expand their capacity to create the results they truly desire"* and where people are continually learning how to learn together (Senge, 2004:2). Senge notes that *"learning organizations are possible because, deep down, we are all learners"* (Senge, 2004:8).

So, in the learning organization, where customer centricity development will be one of the key priorities, the employees will get an opportunity to upgrade their necessary skills on a continuous basis. Such an approach will doubtlessly allow continuous development and improvement of the CX, which will have a direct positive impact on the customers' satisfaction rate, and, consequently, on the company's stable development.

It is also necessary to pay attention to the organizational culture, which is one of key conditions for the creation of a customer-centered company (Fader and Toms, 2018; Peppers and Rogers, 2011). A direct link between organizational culture and the effectiveness of company's work is recognized both by business and by academic science (Basch, 2002; Kotter and Heskett, 1992 in Bartley et al. 2007).

Robin and Judge (2013) state that the organizational culture represents a common perception the organization's members hold and produces the most direct impact on all the company's employees. Consequently, customer-centered culture will produce an invaluable impact on maintaining and development of relevant skills of the company employees and will send an explicit signal to new employees that a customer is the top value of the company. According to Khan (no data), *"...customer centric organization is where every process starts and ends with customer satisfaction in mind. It's a culture, not an event"*.

It is necessary to note that to maintain customer centricity at an adequate level, the personnel must have a clear understanding of the link between personal success and the observation of the customer-centered policy. Thus, it is very important to encourage relevant transactions, when the employees' customer-centered behavior will be motivated by bonuses, rise of basic wages, career growth, and other subcomponents. Raven (1997) remarks that motivation is the key factor encouraging people's professional development and activity.

According to Berry (1995), the personnel's customer centricity depends also on hiring. Yohn (2018) emphasizes that *"from the very first interaction with prospective employees, organizations should make thinking about customers and their needs a clear priority"*. It is stated that some people are inclined to anticipate and realize their new experience, related to focusing on the customer's needs independently, while the others would prefer a more traditional work environment, with someone telling them what to do (Markey and Reichheld, 2013). That is why the task of recruiting is to define people preferring the first behavior pattern, already at the stage of shortlisting.

It should be stressed that the effectiveness of CX, facilitating the creation of customer value, directly depends on the collective work of the whole company's personnel and departments. This is manifested by the practical example of the General Electric. It is stated in this company that when all the personnel and, consequently, all departments work as a single unit, it gives much better results (Baker, 2017).

One of the conditions for a successful personnel collaboration is the percolation of systems thinking principles in a company (Senge, 2004). Jones (2012) observes that systems thinking is *"the DNA of collaboration"*.

The core idea of systems thinking is that it, being based on the principles of holism, considers the whole, not as a simple set of interrelated elements but as a system consisting of cooperating elements that influence one another (Ackoff, 1999; Jackson, 2003). As any company is a set of departments and functions, it can be considered as a system; this means that the application of systems thinking principles to a company is perfectly reasonable. The integration of holistic principles and systems thinking facilitates more productive decision of the tasks that the company accomplishes and an integrated work of all the company's constituents (Jackson, 2003).

The main difference of a system, built on holistic principles, from a system uniting both the principles of holisms and the principles of systems thinking is as follows: in the first case, all elements will be interconnected, and in the second case there will also be a constant systems cooperation between them.

For instance, active cooperation of such sub-branches as sales, marketing, and service will help in more effective shaping of a value proposition for the customers (KPMG, 2017). Being based on the systems thinking principles, their collective work may look like this: the Marketing Department, on the basis of the market analysis, formulates the customers' requirements for the company's product or service. Then these requirements are discussed with the Department of Sales and Service. As the result of this work, the optimal customer value proposition is formed. In the given case, not a mere information exchange takes place but the discussion of information with collective development of optimal decisions. Senge (2004) emphasizes that systems thinking has inter-disciplinary characteristics, it facilitates the optimal issue solutions, and it also creates new knowledge.

According to Hamrefors (2010), an organization is a communication unit, where, as the result of mutual cooperation and communications, the best value proposition is formed, which meets the customers' needs.

Systems thinking also presupposes that a change in one part of the system must touch upon all its other parts; in the contrary case, the system's effective work will be complicated (Ackoff at al., 2010). For instance, the introduction of a new product onto the market must be accompanied by the change in existing communications with the customers, perhaps, by the changes in the approach to maintenance service. In the contrary case, the company will not be able to create a real value proposition for the customers.

For a successful realization of systems thinking, managers should understand what is common among various parts of the company and how they can act collectively (Ackoff et al., 2010). For instance, the vision, determining the customer to be number one priority of the company, can serve as an indisputable and unifying pointer in the process of decision making for all departments in the company.

The key role in systems thinking development will certainly be played by the company's leader and its top management who must demonstrate the systems approach to work and delivery of solutions by setting a personal example (Martens, 2001).

An important role is also given to training, aimed at systems thinking development in the company personnel, their target being the upgrading of cooperation, for creating and realization of effective CX (Pourdehnad et al., 2011).

The systems approach can also be transferred onto the company's cooperation with its stakeholders, when common grounds and common goals are sought collectively, and the systems work begins so as to achieve them and generate values for each other. Thus, a customer-centered leader and personnel and their cooperation form the foundation for the creation of a customer-centered company and the development of its unique CX.

To ensure the fullest participation of personnel in CX creation and execution, companies should pay attention to the development of the employees' customer centricity skills, provide the relevant motivation, and grant the employees the opportunity of direct influence on CX. Besides, the presence of the corresponding corporate culture is needed, as well as of the customer-centered vision and values, which guide the employees while taking decisions. Because of this approach the company will be able to ensure personnel's participation in the creation of best CX and in providing it to the customers in the most effective way.

Integrated Marketing

The principle of holism is also applied in the process of realizing the next holistic marketing element – the integrated marketing, which presupposes the creation of integrated marketing communications with the customers. Smith and Zook (2011) note that all online and offline marketing channels of customer communications must also be united by a common concept and a common idea, which considerably expand the company's customer centricity rate and raise loyalty to its brand.

A vivid example of integrated marketing communications is Reebok's advertising campaign united by one slogan: *"Be more human"* (Adidas, 2018:70). The main target of this campaign is the creation of the customers' emotional link with the Reebok brand. This motto, encouraging people to believe in themselves, served as a platform for the Reebok's further advertising activity: *"the platform supported by several relevant assets and influencers in the digital ecosystems"* (Adidas, 2018:70). The company invited well-known female athletes who *"told their personal stories about overcoming barriers to become their best selves"*, created a clothing line united by the slogan *"Be more human"*, and was active in placing its information in online social networks using offline channels as well (Adidas, 2018:70, Reebok, no data). Simultaneously, the company organized sports contests for local communities' residents, during which they were encouraged to develop their self-confidence (Bemorehuman, 2019).

According to Shimp (2010), integrated marketing communications not only distinguish the company from its competitors but also produce a positive impact on its profit. For instance, the *"Be more human"* initiative, starting in 2015, had its impact on the Reebok brand's net sales, having enlarged this index by about 11% (Adidas, 2013, 2015, 2016; Statista, 2019).

Blakeman (2018) emphasizes that integrated marketing communications must correspond to the needs of the whole target audience; at the same time, they must be personalized, meeting the needs of an individual customer, delivering valuable information on the company's product or service. This approach facilitates the creation of long-term relations between the company and its customers (Blakeman, 2018).

Considering the strategic importance of integrated communications, they must be carefully planned and implemented and their effectiveness must be measured (Juska, 2018). The plan of creating the integrated marketing communication may contain the following elements (Juska, 2018):

- the targets to be achieved;
- the budget for the creation of integrated marketing communication;
- the concept of information delivery to the customer;
- communication channels;
- the implementation program; and
- indicators allowing the measurement of target achievement success.

Besides, any planning of marketing communications must begin with determining the customers' requirements and wishes, because it is their voice that is a strategically important starting point for the creation of effective communications.

It is necessary to note that if the company's personnel do not support the communicated plot, the efforts invested for creating positive customer links will fail (Smith and Zook, 2011). For instance, if the company guarantees a prompt delivery of the ordered products, it will not receive necessary results without the introduction of relevant changes in the personnel's work. This fact is another support for stressing personnel's strategic importance for the customer-centered company to work effectively.

Thus, integrated marketing communication performs several important functions:

- Differentiate the company in its competitive line
- Effectively inform potential customers on the value they receive by cooperating with the company
- Facilitate the setting of long-term customer bonds
- Make a positive impact on the profit.

Product or Service Marketing

So, all integrated communication channels, as well as the cooperation of all departments and the personnel of the company, follow a single target: the creation of a valuable customer experience. However, this is impossible without a relevant product or service, which solves the customer's problems in the best way. Newman (2016) remarks that *"customer journey starts with product conception"*.

For instance, Adidas (2018:19) declares that their wish to be *"the best sports company in the world"* directly depends on their customers' love of their products. Procter & Gamble (2019) lay the stress on the fact that their products are one of the main reasons for their success, as they form the customers' positive attitude on the brand.

But a product can as easily make a company the customers' favorite as it can create serious problems for the company. In August 2016, a new smartphone appeared on the market. It was the Samsung's flagship product – Galaxy Note 7 (GSM Arena, no data). However, in September, the company faced the necessity of recalling this product because of serious problems with accumulators and had to stop the sale completely (BBC, 2017; Samsung, 2017). As estimated by Samsung (2017), about 97% out of 3.06 million units of sold Galaxy Note 7 were recalled. The expenses related to recalling this variant of smartphones cost the company about $5.3 billion (Lopez, 2017).

D. J. Koh, President of Mobile Communications Business for Samsung, stated that the company would undertake all possible measures to restore the trust for the brand (Lopez, 2017). And it appears that Samsung made serious conclusions from this incident, having announced that *"product safety comes before everything"* (Samsung, 2017:43). In 2017 the company introduced new initiatives facilitating the improvement of its product quality, as, for instance, *"Eight-Point Battery Safety Checklist"*, raising the control level of "accumulators production" (Samsung, 2017:43).

Besides the prompt response to the situation with improper accumulators, one of the factors of Samsung's restoration, as experts noted, was the appearance of a new successful flagship product S8 (Lee and Athavaley, 2017; Tsukayama, 2017). Rash (2017) observes that for Samsung, S8 is more than a smartphone; it is the thing with the help of which Samsung *"needs to get its good name back"*. Thus, Samsung's products can be quite understandably considered to be the reason of Samsung's fall and the mover of its growth. In the given case, these are two flagship smartphones – Galaxy S7 and Galaxy S8.

The example explained above is a very clear illustration for the idea that the key issue of customer centricity is a company's product or service. It is the product that is the company's ambassador, the foundation for the company's cooperation with its customers, and for creating its reputation. Any mistakes in the product will weaken the company's position considerably. Freeman (2016:9) states that the key element that forms the basis for customer centricity itself is *"great products and services for customers"*. The company must give its product the most careful attention, considering it to be an essential element of customer centricity.

At the same time, it is necessary to note that this does not mean that a company is transformed into a customer-centered one once everything is concentrated around its product or service. According to Hemel and Rademakers (2016:213), a company must preserve its commitment to customer centricity on the basis of the postulate that *"deeply understanding customers' needs first, and only then do they start developing products, services or solutions"*. This opinion is also shared by Gorchels (2000:16) who states that a company must be governed exclusively by a customer's voice if it *"strives to create competitively superior products and services"*. For instance, GE created two specialized "Customer Experience Centers", where cooperation and communication with the customers on a wide range of questions takes place (General Electric, 2017).

Today, many companies have begun to take an active interest in what are true customer requirements and how they can meet those requirements in the best way (McKinsey & Company, 2017).

This question can be answered with such a tool as 4A marketing, the main purpose of which is value creation for the customers and other company's stakeholders (Sheth and Sisodia, 2012). The 4 A's of marketing allows creating a value proposition based on the most important value characteristics of a product or service – *Acceptability, Affordability, Accessibility, and Awareness* – which are given a thorough description in Table 4.1 (Sheth and Sisodia, 2012).

Table 4.1 4A marketing components

Value	Acceptability	Product or service proposition must meet the customers' requirements and expectations or exceed them
Value component	Functional acceptability	Functions of product/service, its reliability and quality must correspond to the customer's expectations.
	Psychological acceptability	The company's product must induce positive emotions of potential and current customers.
Value	Affordability	Product or service proposition must correspond to customers' financial capacities, as well as to their wish to pay for the suggested product/service
Value component	Economic acceptability	The suggested product/service must correspond to the customers' financial capacities.
	Psychological acceptability	Product/service must induce the desire to pay for obtaining it.
Value	Accessibility	All conditions must be created for the customers' easy purchase of the product/service
Value component	Availability	In offering a product/service, the company must be sure of its ability to meet the customer demand.
	Convenience	The company must ensure the availability of product/ service for the customers.
Value	Awareness	Current or potential customers must be well enough informed of the suggested product or service
Value component	Product knowledge	Potential customers will make purchases more likely if they have adequate positive information on the suggested product or service.
	Brand awareness	Potential customers will make purchases more likely if they have adequate positive information on the company brand.

Generated from Sheth and Sisodia (2012).

The use of the 4A marketing offers companies a unique opportunity of considering all nuances in the process of creating a product or service, forming a top-value proposition. It is necessary to note that the 4A marketing is a holistic approach to the formation of the customer value based on the customer's requirements. Consequently, all components are interrelated, and lack of attention to any one of them may have a negative influence on the company's ability to satisfy the customer's requirements.

Product or service marketing is the key component of CX. Thus, this marketing concept, which has the main target of generating customer value by means of a product or a service, will play an important strategic role in creating a positive CX for the company. The facts introduced provide all grounds for the correction of holistic marketing by including the product or service marketing into its structure; this will allow companies to execute their marketing activity more effectively, creating and developing CX.

Relationship Marketing

Berry (1995) noted that the company's quality product or service, which meets the customers' requirements completely, is a key element of relationship marketing, allowing the creation of effective long-term customer relationships.

So, relationship marketing presupposes the existence and development of mutually beneficial long-term relations between the company and the customer, which in sum produces a positive effect upon the company's profit (Peck et al., 2004). Andersen (2011) emphasizes that the company must follow its customers' wishes and respond by the best solutions to their issues and problems.

However, despite all the company's efforts in building firm links with its customers, a business annually loses about 20% of its customers on average (Galetto, 2017). This data is confirmed by the estimation of the customer churn in the following US industries: cable, retail, financial, online retail, telecom, and travel. The average customer outflow in the stated industries is 23% (Statista, 2020). Customers are often not inclined to demonstrate their brand devotion even in the event of complete satisfaction with their cooperation with the company, exercising the so-called customer migration (Ang and Buttle, 2010; Li et al., 2016).

It is reported that the most consequential reason of customer churn is observed in cases when customers *"switch from one company to another"* (Tate, 2020). According to Buttle and Maklan (2015), the lost customers must be substituted by new ones. But according to Berry (1995:236), *"the attraction of new customers should be viewed only as an intermediate step in the marketing process"*. Berry (1995:244) states that relationship marketing can *"help firms attract more new customers"*, as the current customers will spread information about the company.

> Thus, within relationship marketing, the key role in attracting new customers is given to the "word of mouth". "Word of mouth" is rather an efficient tool for spreading the information about the company.
>
> (Whitler, 2014)

According to Kumar et al. (2007), the value of a customer lies not only in the fact that he can buy but also in what he would say about the company.

However, information can also be negative; moreover, it can be spread further also in the case when the company has overcome some negative moment in its activity. According to the customer satisfaction research, a *"satisfied customer tells eight people"* about his or her negative customer experience, *"whereas a dissatisfied customer tells 22"* (Lakshmi, 2013).

As it can be seen, the most vulnerable point of relationship marketing is that this concept considers new customer acquisition not to be its main function. It should be noted that if a company wants to enlarge its market presence, to introduce a new product or service, to raise the purchase rate, and to ensure its further development, a close attention should be paid to acquisition of new customers (Ang and Buttle, 2010; Zhang, 2019). It is emphasized that if a company does not pay due attention to customer acquisition, a failure is its most likely future (Direct Marketing Association, 2014).

Thus, customer retention, as well as customer acquisition, must be the important component of relationship marketing. By combining retention and acquisition, companies create their reliable sales market: they can not only compensate for natural customer migration but also move toward the expansion of their market, which is a critically important condition for the development of any company.

The process of customer acquisition, as well as customer retention, starts with careful planning and answering the question, who is the company's customer and what are his or her needs and requirements (Bracks, 2012). In general, the creation of stable customer bonds and customer retention and acquisition must be realized on the basis of the following principles:

1   To create an effective system of integrated marketing communications and advertising, facilitating the acquisition of new customers, as well as the retention of the current ones.
2   To propose only safe products and services that add value.
3   To respond timely to customer requirements.
4   To consider the customer voice in creating products or services.
5   To build customer relations only on the grounds of following legal and ethical norms, of mutual trust and transparency.
6   To provide quality and timely service.

A company can launch its search for new customers by proposing its product or service and integrated communications at its current market as well as at new ones. Besides, the success of a modern company rests on its cooperation not only with its customers but also with other key stakeholders.

Freeman and Velamuri (2005) emphasize that it is rather difficult for companies to build effective customer relations without building similar relations with other stakeholders. It is stated that the creation of a product or service that *"customers want to buy"* requires the consideration of requirements of the following stakeholders (Freeman, 2016:9):

- *Suppliers*, who strive to make the business better by supplying quality products or services;
- *Employees*, who both provide the creation of a product/service and are responsible for the company's CX;
- *Communities*; in case their wishes for the company's activity are neglected, restrictive measures can be introduced, which hinder the conducting of business.

The interests of owners, investors, and shareholders must be considered too. This stakeholder can restrict the company's activity in the event that they disagree with its strategy, or if the value proposition, which first of all is associated in this group with the profit, is absent (Carrol and Buchholtz, 2009).

Similarly, stakeholders are identified as strategic and important for the success of the company by such global business giants as Adidas (2018), Samsung (2017), and Tesco (2016). The relationship with each of the named stakeholders will be considered separately.

Suppliers

It is necessary to pay attention to the fact that the companies like Tesco (2016), General Electric (2018), and Samsung (2018) characterize the relations with their suppliers by giving them the rank of strategic significance. All these three companies demonstrate a high level of integration and bonds with their suppliers, strictly observing ethical standards as far as their partners are concerned.

Samsung (2018) states that they see their suppliers as their key partners and that they are going to constantly invest in the development of these bilateral and mutually beneficial relations. General Electric created a special Internet portal for their suppliers – gesupplier.com.

Tesco (2016:6) demonstrates that as the result of their mutual work with their suppliers they managed to develop a *"more efficient and sustainable way of working"* and the *"average weekly shop"* for customers was reduced by 3%. Among the improvements, suggested by Tesco for the suppliers, definite terms of request processing were worked out and a support line was created. A new approach to cash payments was adopted; the ethical code for supplier relations was developed. Besides, to support productive relations with suppliers, the Supplier Network was created numbering over 5,000 members. The example of Tesco is a clear evidence of the idea that positive relations and value-generating activities for suppliers, on the side of the company, may have the most positive influence on CX, and consequently, on the company's development.

Employees

The company's personnel are the key stakeholders, on whom the company's product or service quality, the process of customer retention or acquisition, and consequently, the whole CX of the company depend directly (Subramanian, 2017). The survey of the opinions of customers of hotels show that they are not at all indifferent to the relations existing between the company and its employees, and the better these relations are the more satisfied the customers are (Glassdoor, 2017).

According to Clarke and Kinghorn (2018), a great majority of companies (71%) are sure that their employees produce a considerable impact on the CX. However, the most efficient contribution to the company's development is made by its engaged personnel (Kruse, 2012; Vance, 2006).

To engaged personal, according to Vance (2006), belong motivated employees, who use maximum efforts for the solution of tasks, facilitating the achievement of the company's targets. According to Gallup (2016), engaged employees facilitate the company's development more effectively.

Engaged employees identify themselves with the company, and they feel "emotional commitment" to the organization and its goals, which influences positively both the term of their work and the relationship with the company (Kruse, 2012). According to Berry (1995), the longer employees work in the company, the more experience they have for the relationships with the customers, which positively influences the customer centricity rate.

The organization must continuously develop employee engagement, which requires *"two-way relationship between employer and employee"* and is an important condition for realizing relationship marketing (Vance, 2006:3). For instance, in Tesco (2017:74), the company is systematically working at the improvement of bilateral communication channels with its employees to ensure a prompt response to their comments and *"to ensure they are engaged in the decisions we make for the business"*. In the company, the "employee engagement network" is created, facilitating the personnel's development and retention, by means of various initiatives, like *"career sponsorship, mentoring and networking"* (Tesco-careers, no data). Besides, much attention is given to the improvement of the payment and reward plan.

The created internal colleague networks deserve special attention, such as "Women at Tesco", "Armed Forces at Tesco", and others, *"which provide support to allow colleagues to be themselves at work and develop within Tesco"* (Tesco, 2018:27). Thus, the company creates all conditions for its employees to feel their bond with it and to be engaged in the current events and to be able to influence them. Tesco (2019:80) notes that engaging the personnel allows the company to be *"closest to our customers"*.

It is necessary to observe that general employee engagement is an important but an insufficient condition for effective CX creation (Pacific Consulting Group, 2018; Yohn, 2018). Companies must develop the personnel engagement directly into creative activity and realization of CX, which creates value for the company's customers.

It is stated that in most successful companies, the number of employees engaged in the realization of the principle "customer first" constitutes 50% and demonstrates the upward trend (Pacific Consulting Group, 2018). For the purpose of employee engagement in the realization of the "customer first" principle, into the CX creation and realization, attention should be focused on the following drivers (Pacific Consulting Group, 2018):

1 *Willingness* – the employee self-motivation, which finds its expression in a sincere desire to create and realize the effective experience for the customers;
2 *Ability* – the facilitation from the company management for the realization of a customer-centered approach, which finds expression in the following:
   • providing the employees opportunity for proposing and realizing ideas, leading to CX improvement;
   • the employees' feedback for realizing the effectiveness of the CX;
   • the existence of trust- and transparency-based relationships in the company;
   • timely and quality solutions of problems hindering the CX creation and its realization;
   • the employees obtaining a due recognition rate in the process of their task solution related to customer centricity.
3 *Management support* – the existence of the necessary technical facilities for the effective CX creation and realization:
   • the existence of the necessary non-faulty operative equipment for the maintenance of service provision;
   • the existence of necessary communication channels to converse with the customers.

To provide the best employee engagement for the creation and development of CX, the top management must constantly focus their attention on the thesis that customer centricity is the key priority for the company's development (Yohn, 2018).

It should be noted that on the basis of holism principles for the interconnection of a system's parts, it is important to emphasize that without giving due attention to general engagement, the company will hardly be able to mold an adequate employee engagement rate into CX creation.

Society

Carrol and Buchholtz (2009) stress that today's business and society are inextricably linked, and they influence one another's development not only by trade relations. For instance, Adidas (2017) states that by means of sports they can exercise a most direct and positive influence on the whole society. Thanks to Adidas' (2018:69) initiative, throughout the whole world, *"close to a million runners were activated to raise fund and awareness for the fight against ocean plastic through Run for the Ocean"*. Besides, Adidas (2017) participates in the global program aimed at the prevention of noxious air emissions.

Samsung (2017) also takes an active part in the improvement of environment by creating their own program named Climate Change Response Strategy; its signification is the realization of initiatives leading to the improvement of ecological situation. Nielsen (2018) states that the number of respondents who want to have as their partners the companies that take care of the environment runs to 81%.

One of Tesco's (2016) projects "Eat Happy/Farm to Fork" was aimed at demonstrating the advantages of healthy eating. In 2015, the project reached its peak, as over one million children took part in it (Tesco, 2016). Besides, Tesco (2016), to promote the healthy way of life, conducts joint projects with "Diabetes UK" and the "British Heart Foundation". By these projects, Tesco confidently demonstrates their contribution to the society's development, showing the advantages of healthy living and eating. Simultaneously, the sales data testify to the fact that Tesco's total organic food sales increased 15% on average (Atherton, 2017).

Dave Lewis (2017), Tesco Group Chief Executive, notes that the care for customers' health and the offer of healthy foods for them considerably raised the customers' loyalty for the Tesco brand. Initiatives of such kind belong to cause-related marketing, when the company involves potential customers in direct or indirect participation in mutually beneficial actions facilitating "revenue-producing" outcomes (Kottler and Keller, 2016).

Thus, a company, by exercising close cooperation with society, can receive not only its customers' approval but also increasingly strident financial dividends.

Shareholders

A special mention must be made on building effective relations with shareholders, investors, and owners. Carrol and Buchholtz (2009) state that the voice of this stakeholders must be heard as it is obligatory. For instance, owners want reporting relationships on the company's side regarding business and the company's financial activity and meeting the demand that business must give profits (Carrol and

Buchholtz, 2009). Golding (2014) remarks that, without any doubt, "businesses need shareholders, but they need customers more".

Ohtonen (2015) emphasizes that the company's profit and success depend on the customer completely *"because customers are the source of revenue"*. This is proved true by such a key index of the company's work effectiveness as the "gross profit margin". This ratio demonstrates profitability in relation to sales, and its result completely depends on the amount of products, which was bought by the customers (Brigham and Houston, 2015).

So, the main task of the company's top management is to turn shareholders, investors, and owners into the company's allies in building a customer-centered company. The grounds for this slogan is simple: the customer is the basis for the company's profit, and investments into customer centricity development will no doubt facilitate its growth.

In sum, the foregoing analysis shows the importance of relationship marketing concept for the successful creation and realization of effective CX. Due to successful customer bonds, the company provides a reliable sales market for itself through the skill of attracting new customers. The activity of engaged employees will produce the most positive impact on the company's CX. Mutually beneficial relations with suppliers will help the company in the formation of the most valuable proposition for its customers. Investing into the development of the society and local communities, the company will not only create its good reputation but will be able to convert it into profit. The existing business relations with shareholders and meeting their demands will help the company in the realization of its definite development paths in achieving its goals.

According to Freeman and Velamuri (2005), a company generating value for all the parties concerned will more likely transform this approach into a successful financial result.

Performance Marketing

Alongside this customer centricity, the creation of effective customer experience and the development of bonds with stakeholders require sizable investments by the company. Adidas (2018) states that they constantly broaden their marketing investments aimed at the creation of stable connections with various sport clubs, athletes, and sport federations, which are their potential customers. Samsung invests measurable sums into the development of its suppliers' competitiveness. In 2017 the expenses on teaching suppliers were about $7 million (Samsung, 2017).

So, the use of performance marketing, presuming, according to Kotler and Keller (2016:47), the understanding of *"financial and nonfinancial returns"* from marketing activities, is seen as a critically important element. Companies must understand how effective their investments into the CX development were and to what extent their key stakeholder – the customer – as well as other stakeholders are satisfied with their cooperation with the company. Besides, the company must get the answer to the main question: did the marketing activity really facilitate the improvement of financial positions in the shape of obtaining necessary profit?

However, according to Smith (2018), the company will expect its profit only on the condition of its customer motivated by its proposition to spend his or her money. Also, a customer needs something more than simple satisfaction of his or her requirement in exchange for the money that he or she has spent (Weinstein and Elison, 2012). A customer needs value, which he or she expects from his cooperation with the company (Weinstein and Elison, 2012).

According to Anderson and Narus (1998), value in business means technical, economic, service, and social benefits received by a customer in exchange of the price he pays for a market proposition. And yet, Weinstein and Elison (2012) emphasize that value is not simply the provision of service, quality, image, and an attractive price for a product or service but the company's extraordinary efforts facilitating full satisfaction of the customer's requirements.

According to Baer (2016), great customer experience occurs only in the event of the company managing to exceed the customer's expectations. A poor customer experience is the result of the company's inability to meet the customer's expectations (Baer, 2016).

The connection between customer satisfaction and positive results of business activity are well known (Anderson et al., 1997). Weinstein and Elison (2012) observe that the more attractive value proposition the company manages to form for customers, the more likely is the chance of achieving the high financial indicators.

Apple is the company that has built CX based on exceptional customer value proposition. In 2007, Apple offered its customers an innovative smartphone – iPhone with a new operating system (*Encyclopedia Britannica*, 2019). The unique product was supplied with a no less unique service, which included (Fisk et al., 2014):

1   A website, providing information on the product and its maintenance service;
2   Apple retail stores, presenting the possibility of customers' independent acknowledgment of iPhone and other company's products;
3   iTunes – music store; after registering in it and loading a special application, an iPhone owner could download music and listen to it; App store – the Internet store where users could download various applications, which could be installed on the iPhone;
4   iCloud – a cloud storage from Apple where users could keep backup copies of information placed on the iPhone and the iPad.

Certainly, not all of these services were provided by the company simultaneously. But its customers saw that the company cared for their convenience by continuously suggesting to them new decisions, which added value to its products. Moreover, Apple also suggested a new format for the producers of smartphone accessories. Thus, iPhone owners had an opportunity to get carrying cases of various colors and shapes for their smartphone. Due to this approach, customers were offered a unique chance of outer personalization of their iPhones, which was also an innovative decision, adding value to the product.

Besides, Apple offered its customers not only a product and a service of exceptional quality but also an image of belonging to a special cohort of people possessing Apple's technical appliances. It is noted that possessing an iPhone allowed people to have at their disposal *"the shiny new thing, the one that everyone's talking about"* (Matyszczyk, 2018). Between the company's brand and its customers there appeared a strong emotional and psychological bond (Lewis, 2014). It is worth noting that customers, who are emotionally connected with the brand, buy more products or services of this brand, they are less touchy about the change of prices, and they often recommend this brand to other people and are more willing to communicate with the company (Zorfas and Leemon, 2016).

It is possible to state that Apple exceeded its customers' expectations by creating a proposition of the top value due to its innovative product and service. For instance, during the second quarter of 2018, Apple, with its general market share of 12.1%, received 62% of global cellphone market's profits (Statista, 2018, 2019). It should also be added that in the "Best Global Brands 2018 Rankings" rating, which shows the rating of brands, to which customers demonstrate the greatest loyalty, Apple takes the first place (Interbrand, 2018).

Thus, due to a well-executed innovative value proposition, Apple, which does not possess a meaningful market share, generates profit thanks to the existence of its loyal customers. It is stated in Apple that the company *"is committed to bringing the best user experience to its customers through its innovative hardware, software, peripherals, and services"* (Apple, Inc., 2018:1).

Surely, not all companies can propose such bright value solutions as they do in Apple. Nevertheless, any company can offer to its customers *"positively improving existing products or services"* (Fan et al., 2017:1). For instance, Samsung (2017), in its annual report, noted not only what the company had done for "customer value enhancement", but it also declared its plans for the future. Thus, in 2016–17, the company achieved "Product Quality and Safety", having created the Global Quality Innovation Division. It also developed more demanding standards of quality and safety and offered a more comfortable service for people with special needs (Samsung, 2017).

For the years ahead, Samsung connects their "Customer Value Enhancement" with the "Continued Innovation of the Quality Assurance System" program and with continuous development of the customers' maintenance service (Samsung, 2017).

So, before it defines the realization of success of CX in the framework of its whole marketing activity, a company must be sure that it really offers the customers a valuable solution to their requirements. In other words, a company should exercise the planning of its CX and define the ways of its realization.

Nicholas and Steyn (2012) emphasize that planning and control cannot exist without each other. According to Mone et al. (2013), performance marketing is not only the assessment of the obtained results but also the planning and execution of necessary actions. Thus, in the performance marketing framework, both the planning of CX planning, CX execution, and CX assessment must be exercised.

It is necessary to note that CX planning must completely correlate with the general strategy of the company's development; it must be an integral part of this strategy. This will allow shaping a value proposition for the customers in the most effective way depending on the chosen strategy. For instance, having determined the further development strategy with the help of Ansoff (2007) matrix, a company will find a more appropriate approach to CX planning and realization:

Market penetration means the expansion of traditional markets with the help of the current product line:

• Value proposition on the basis of the current product/service is developed; probably, its correction according to customers' opinion is necessary for a more effective implementation of customer retention and acquisition.
• Effective communication channels are necessary, which stimulate repeat purchases by existing customers as well as facilitate customer acquisition on the current market.

Product development means the presentation of modified or new products on the current market:

• Feeding upon customers' opinions, it is necessary to develop a value proposition on the basis of modified or new products.
• Effective communication channels are necessary, facilitating the purchases of new or modernized products both by existing, and new customers.

Market development means that a strategy presupposes the exploration of new markets for current products:

• The value proposition on the basis of the current product is developed; perhaps, its modification based on customers' opinion on new markets is necessary for more effective exercising of customer acquisition.
• Effective communication channels are necessary, facilitating customer acquisition for purchasing the company's products on new markets.

Diversification means entering new markets with new products:

• It is necessary to develop a value proposition for new markets based on new products and the requirements of potential customers.
• Effective communication channels are necessary, facilitating customers' acquisition for purchasing the company's products on new markets.

Besides, within the value planning framework, it is necessary to draw up a budget related to realizing CX, as the company's financial resources are not limitless. The expenses on CX realization must also be governed within the company's budget policy framework. It is stated that as customer centricity is becoming an increasingly more meaningful trend, many companies will have to create a centralized function to govern this process, which also requires a corresponding budget and resources (Hyken, 2018).

According to Parker (2018), budgeting is the key issue for the financial success of a company, as its usage helps the company to achieve its financial targets in the best way. Because the company expects the improvement of its financial indices resulting from CX application, the usage of a corresponding budget, facilitating the CX development, is seen as extremely necessary. The use of budgeting will allow (Parker, 2018; Shim et al., 2012):

- formalizing of all targets and plans for CX creation and realization;
- controlling of the expenditure;
- considering the search of alternative decisions;
- the assessment of CX effectiveness.

It is necessary to note that items of budget expenditure must consider the interconnection of all processes in the company. Investments into the upgrading of CX digitalization, which is a necessary condition for improvements in the company's communication opportunities, must be accompanied by investments related to personnel development. As the solution of only technical side of this issue appears insufficient, the company must alter the employees' mentality, spreading digital transformation all through the company. Consequently, it is necessary to finance the introduction of corresponding teaching programs for the personnel.

Besides, it is necessary to invest into research and development, facilitating continuous CX improvement. According to Bozeman and Melkers (1993:1), research and development is a critically important factor for *"productivity, productivity growth and innovations"*. It is noted that a key issue related to research in the CX sphere is the understanding of the idea who the company's customers are and what their needs are, and what are the means of maintaining communications with the customers for offering them the best value solution (Selden and MacMillan, 2006).

It is essential to place an emphasis on the fact that today's world is very instable and unpredictable (Whitley, 2006). Customer satisfaction rate also is a dynamically varying phenomenon, and its downswing may produce a negative influence on the company's success. In such a situation, planning as a tool may happen to be ineffective and may require immediate correction due to a changed situation.

Consequently, the company must be able to take instant measures aimed at the correcting the situation. In the given case, a prompt correction of earlier planned actions is required using *"real-time responses or decision making with Big Data"* (Galar and Kumar, 2017; Taylor, 2014).

The root of the stated methodology is that continuous monitoring of certain indices, related to the company's activity, will help in prompt reacting, in the event the situation changes for the worse. Having developed the indicators that characterize the effectiveness of CX realization and tracing their dynamic changes, the company can promptly work out the plan of correction activities, facilitating the solution for the current situation.

Thus, within the performance marketing framework, the company must keep track of the change in the dynamics of indicators, not only for defining the CX effectiveness but also for promptly reacting to the change in the situation.

According to Moore (2019), the change in the company's CX realization will enable conducting an analysis of the effectiveness of investments made and actions undertaken, determining future targets/aims and tasks and correcting the current situation. It is possible to do this on the basis of such indices as key performance indicators (KPI) and metrics.

- KPI is the index allowing to learn how efficient were the company's efforts aimed at the achievement of its target goal (Alsadeq and Hakam, 2010).
- Metrics are the indicators helping to keep track of the performance and progress while the target is being achieved (O'Hara and Ginger, 2000).

An example of KPI, measuring the efficiency of CX realization, can be customer satisfaction (CSAT). This is the most traditional index, which is calculated on the basis of customer survey or on the basis of indirect indicators, like opinions of the company's product, service offered, and general impressions about the received CX (Moore, 2019). If the percentage of satisfied customers is rather high and tends to 100%, keeping its positive dynamics, it can show that the company's targets of effective CX creation are achieved at a certain stage (Gandy and Toister, 2017).

The strategic importance of this KPI is explained by the fact that the main target of the company's CX is full satisfaction or anticipation of the customer's requirements by forming a value proposition. To give an example of metrics, demonstrating the company's progress with regard to the achievement of its key targets related to customer centricity, such an indicator can be suggested as the company's capacity to provide products and services of the quality, timeliness, and expenses that are agreed with the customers (O'Hara and Ginger, 2000). This indicator produces a direct influence on CSAT, as a quality and timely product or service delivery is the factor of top importance influencing the customer's satisfaction rate. For instance, Adidas (2018) applies the methodology of On-Time-in-Full (OTIF), allowing to estimate the speed and quality of product delivery to customers, and consequently, it has its impact on the customer satisfaction rate.

Besides, as the metrics showing how successfully the company's CX is being realized, the following indicators can be used (Fader and Toms, 2018; Kotler and Keller, 2016):

- *Customer churn rate*: It is used to determine the number of people who stopped being the company's customers in a certain period of time. The uptick of this indicator rate requires the company's prompt analysis of the situation, stating the reasons that condition the customers' withdrawal from the company, for bringing in correction measures.
- *Net promoter score*: This is the probability rate of customer's recommendation of the company to third parties. It is used for potential probability definition for enlarging the company's customer base.

So, the company, by a continuous monitoring of these metrics, will be able to see the customer satisfaction rate for its services, and in the event of its worsening, may promptly institute suitable correction measures.

It is important to note that customer satisfaction rate also depends on the level of employee engagement into the creation of CX. The need for close attention to this indicator on the company management's side is also stressed (Moore, 2019). It is sensible to include this indicator to the set of key KPIs, influencing the company's CX, as well. The metrics, allowing to understand the employee engagement rate, can be as follows (Pacific Consulting Group, 2018; Wiles, 2018; Yohn, 2018):

- The presence of employees' wish and understanding of following the company's customer-centered values and vision;
- Employees' suggestions for CX improvement;
- Employees' knowledge and opportunities for effective cooperation with the customers;
- Customers' feedback on their cooperation with the company's employees;
- Satisfaction with the cooperation with colleagues for solving a problem in the CX sphere.

Wiles (2018) remarks that the most streamlined method of measuring the employee engagement rate is conducting corresponding surveys from time to time. For instance, in Tesco (2017:32) the employee engagement rate is measured by means of an annual "employee engagement survey". Besides measuring the customer satisfaction and employee satisfaction rates, companies must obligatorily measure the stakeholder satisfaction rate, meaning the stakeholders, influencing the efficiency of CX realization (Kotler and Keller, 2016). Tesco (2016:13), for instance, undertakes regular assessments of supplier satisfaction rate by means of a single question: *"Overall, how satisfied are you with your experience of working with Tesco?"* in their 'Supplier Viewpoint Survey".

It is necessary to note that the company itself should determine which indicators are important for measuring the effectiveness of the realization of CX and the evaluation of stakeholder satisfaction. It is most sensible to create a dashboard, which includes the basic indicators and metrics and is accessible to all the company's employees (Moore, 2019).

The rate of effectiveness of CX realization should be also tracked by indicators, demonstrating the effectiveness of the whole company's work. As an illustrative example, "gross margin" and "sales revenue" can be tracked (Tracy, 2002). Tracy (2002:48) observes that they are in the group of the most important indicators that *"serious investors"* pay attention to. For instance, gross margin, showing the general income from the amount of goods and services sold by the company, is a "starting point for the other profit ratios" (Tracy, 2002:49). Sales revenue shows the income obtained by the company within a definite period from the sale of goods or services (Tracy, 2002). Both indicators are formed by virtue of the activity of the company's customers. Consequently, the more effective the CX offered by the company is, the higher are the gross margin and the sales revenue.

At the same time, there is no direct link between the company's profit and its CX effectiveness (KPMG, 2016). The explanation for this is that the formation of the net profit is influenced by a combination of various factors, such as the sum of paid taxes and the expenses related to the production of goods and creation of service (Hultgren, 1965). However, the low activity of customers produces a strong negative influence on this indicator. So, generally these are very interrelated indicators.

There are also good reasons to periodically conduct a benchmarking analysis, comparing the obtained results not only with similar indicators of your nearest competitors but also with the indicators of those companies that are the best in effective CX creation (Bough et al., 2017). This kind of analysis will effectively assist in the improvement of the company's CX.

In sum, performance marketing is rather a complicated element presuming both planning of the company's marketing activity success, execution, and monitoring, as well as the assessment of effectiveness of actions taken: CX planning, CX execution, CX monitoring, and CX assessment.

Conclusions (Customer Experience Model as a New Marketing Concept)

The analysis done in this chapter showed that for effective CX realization, the company must pay attention to the development, mutual connection, and interaction of such elements as internal marketing, integrated marketing, product or service marketing, relationship marketing, and performance marketing, which includes planning, execution, and monitoring, as well as the measurement of the results obtained. Alongside this, the key role in CX creation is played by the leader of the company, its top management, its personnel, and their successful interaction. Consequently, internal marketing will form the basis for the company's CX, without which its realization is impossible. Its successful realization directly influences the creation of efficient integrated communication channels, the product or service, and stable customer and stakeholder bonds.

There are good reasons to unite all the stated constituents into the customer experience model (CXM). This will allow the company to get a clear understanding of the basic points that must be paid attention to for CX creation. The graphic presentation of this model looks like what is shown in Figure 4.1.

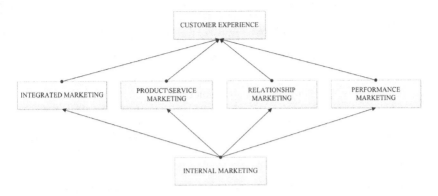

Figure 4.1 The customer experience model.

The main purpose of this model's application is the creation of a unique CX, generating value for the customers and key stakeholders to ensure the necessary profit and a sustainable company development. Table 4.2 gives a full extended presentation of the CXM elements.

Table 4.2 The elements of Customer Experience Model (CXM)

CXM elements	Key points	Goal
Internal marketing	• Customer-centered leader and personnel • Presence of customer-centered vision, value, and culture • Direct personnel's participation in CX creation and development • Personnel's continuous development and motivation • Personnel's cooperation to create effective CX	Creation and realization of the company's CX.
Integrated marketing	• Existing integrated customer communication channels based on the common idea • Information compliance as to the target audience needs • Personalized customer propositions • Planning integrated marketing communication and measuring their effectiveness	Creation of consolidated value proposition for customers by means of integrated communication channels.

(Continued)

CXM elements	Key points	Goal
Product/service marketing	Product/service, meeting the customer's requirements and interests or exceeding them	Creation of customer value proposition by means of the product/service.
Relationship marketing	Existing effective bonds with clients and key stakeholders	• Creation of the company marketing network, consisting of its customers and stakeholders. • Formation of effective bilateral communications "customer company", facilitating both customer retention and customer acquisition. • Provision of continuous employee engagement development as to CX creation and realization.
Performance marketing	CX planning, CX execution and monitoring, CX assessment	CX continuous development and upgrading.

It is necessary to note that the CXM has a number of competitive advantages over holistic marketing:

1   This model is worked out exclusively for the creation of the company's unique CX.
2   CXM closely focuses on the thesis that customer centricity is impossible without the leader who is the protagonist of the given approach, as well as without the leader's cooperation, with the personnel taking an active part in CX creation and realization. So, internal marketing is not an equal ranking CX constituent but its strategic basis. Companies will be targeted on paying the closest attention to their personnel development for the effective CX creation. Only customer-centered personnel can create an effective customer experience!

3   CXM contains product/service marketing as a very important element. Owing to this constituent, while planning its CX, the company will pay the closest attention to the need of considering the customer voice in the process of creation and upgrading of its product/service.

4   A considerable addition is introduced into performance marketing, which presupposes not simply measuring the results but also CX planning and realization and its continuous monitoring of its effectiveness.

Thereby, CXM is seen as a more valuable solution for the CX creation and realization.

5 Empirical Verification of the Customer Experience Model Using the Example of Amazon

This chapter presents an empirical verification of the Customer Experience Model (CXM) using the example of Amazon, the American technology company, which declares customer centricity to be its main strategic priority. As it is noted by the company, Amazon will always follow the *"customer first"* principle and will consider its partners' interests in the most thorough manner to make cooperation *"easier, faster, better, and more cost-effective"* (Amazon, no data; Bezos, 1998).

As it was remarked that *"internal marketing"* is the basis of customer experience, it will be the first element to undergo the empirical verification. The empirical verification of this CXM component, like that of all other components, will be done according to the sequence stated in Table 4.2 and according to each element's key points.

Internal Marketing

Key Points
- Customer-centered leader and personnel
- Customer-centered vision, values, and culture
- Personnel's direct involvement into CX creation and development
- Personnel's continuous development and motivation
- Personnel's cooperation for creating effective CX.

Goal
- Effective creation and execution of the company's CX.

As it was already emphasized, the company's key source of customer centricity is its leader. Thus, the first object of this study is Jeff Bezos, Chairman, President, and CEO of Amazon.com, who founded the company in 1994 (The Amazon blog, no data, Yahoo finance, 2020).

In an interview in 1997, Bezos stressed that the main task for Amazon is the creation of *"real value for the customers"* (Severance, no data). Further, in his first letter to shareholders, Bezos (1997:2; 3) writes that *"from the beginning, our focus has been on offering our customers compelling value"* and *"we will continue to focus relentlessly on our customers"*. So, the attention is focused on the fact that by creating customer value that the company will be able to obtain revenue growth, which is so important for shareholders (Bezos, 1997).

With regard to commitment to customer needs, Bezos talks about it in each of his letters to Amazon's shareholders. For instance, in 1999 Bezos underlined that the company hears its customers, changes, following their interests, and personalizes its propositions with consideration to a definite customer needs (Bezos, 1999).

In his letter to shareholders in 2002, Bezos noted that Amazon would *"continue to drive customer experience"* (Bezos, 2002:1). And finally, in his letter in 2018, Bezos made it perfectly clear again that *"no business could thrive without that kind of customer obsession"* (Bezos, 2018:2). Moreover, each new letter was accompanied by a copy of his first letter in 1997, where Amazon's commitment to customer's needs was proclaimed as the strategic source of the company's profit.

In addition, Bezos defined the vision of the company in 1998, describing Amazon as *"the world's most customer-centric company"* (Bezos, 1998:2). In Amazon's annual report (2017:7), Bezos confirms this vision that all Amazon's actions are determined by its customer-focused approach: *"This year marks the 20th anniversary of our first shareholder letter, and our core values and approach remain unchanged. We continue to aspire to be Earth's most customer-centric company"*.

Bezos (letters 1997–2018) also outlined a clear-cut interpretation of the idea that the company's customer-centered vision must be executed by offering CX to customers, which is grounded on the following:

- Comfortable cooperation of a customer with the company;
- Offering quality product and service at reasonable prices;
- Creation of personalized customer propositions;
- Continuous innovation-based CX development;
- Development of third-party sales on the Amazon platform, aimed at expanding customer propositions;

- Continuous analysis of the "voice of the client" and business development with due consideration of customers' requirements;
- Offering various customer bonuses, for instance, free shipping;
- Creation of the most favorable conditions for the regular customers.

Thus, Bezos can be rightfully considered to be the leader who is the main protagonist of a customer-centered approach.

It is necessary to note that the company's customer-centered vision is shared by its top management. For instance, its Senior Vice President and CFO, Brian Olsavsky, states that the company's success directly depends on its ability to *"keep building more and new tools based on what we're learning from our customers there to better serve in the future"* (Kim, 2018). Amazon Web Services CEO Andy Jassy stresses that he fully shares the company strategy aimed at the customer (CNBC, 2018).

CEO Worldwide Consumer, Jeff Wilke, places an emphasis on the fact that customer centricity development is a continuous process, giving example using artificial intelligence to offer personalized propositions to the company's customers (CNBC, 2019). Further, Wilke points out that while creating new customer possibilities, two sides win: both the customer and the company (Stevens, 2017).

Bezos is sure that only teamwork helps in finding answers to complicated questions and in determining the optimal way for the development of the company (Bloomberg Markets and Finance, 2018). Trust and comfortable relations between Bezos and members of his leadership team are considered to be one of the elements of Amazon's success (Kim, 2019).

Everything suggests that similar behavior and striving to achieve teamwork with the employees are demonstrated also by Amazon's top management. For instance, Shelley Reynolds, Vice President, Worldwide Controller, notes that she continuously analyzes the situation, and seeing the full picture end to end, she communicates with *"a wonderful team, and empowers them to lead"* (AMZ Begin, no data).

Amazon CEO Worldwide Consumer Jeff Wilke remarks that he started his first working day meeting all the members of his team, and already at the end of that day, they confidently shared with him their ideas as to what should be the first thing to be done within the next three months (Amazon News, 2018). Besides, Wilke is sure that during the team discussions, the leader should let the employees speak first; otherwise, there is a great possibility of taking a wrong decision (Amazon News, 2018).

On the whole, in Amazon, they consider their employees to be the basis of CX development. Directly at Jeff Bezos' initiative, thousands of company employees, including Bezos himself, take training within the framework of annual training sessions, in the contact center, communicating with the customers directly, with the purpose of hearing the customers' wishes firsthand (Morgan, 2015).

It is necessary to stress that the company requires the personnel to constantly observe high standards while working with the customers, even when *"no one is watching"* (Bezos, 2017:3). It is stated that high standards begin, first of all, with unconditional performance of one's job responsibilities in the company, with perfect managing of one's profession and requires continuous improvement and development during the whole term of work in the company (Bezos, 2017). It is observing "high standards" of products and services that is an important strategic condition for the CX development (Bezos, 2017).

A vivid example of observing high standards is the company's leader Jeff Bezos. At an early stage of his work in Amazon, Bezos possessed high standards *"on inventing, on customer care, and (thankfully) on hiring"* (Bezos, 2017:1). Later, owing to additional training and cooperation with his colleagues, he mastered high standards on operational process (Bezos, 2017). Bezos notes (2017:1) that a great role in achieving high standards for the company employee is played by two components:

* Continuous training and development, because *"high standards are teachable"*;
* Corporate culture, because *"high standards are contagious."*

To help the employees obtain high standards more effectively, the company is continuously *"investing in education, training, and development"* (Fall, 2019).

For instance, Amazon Technical Academy, created by Amazon software engineers for Amazon employees, is intended to help employees who wish to develop in this sphere (The Amazon blog, no data). The existence of this academy demonstrates the Community of Practice (CoP) in the company, when the employees develop on a collective basis, sharing their knowledge throughout the company.

The given example directly correlates with the principles of "learning organization", in which *"people are continually discovering how they create their reality"* (Senge, 2004:13).

As regards corporate culture, it is important to say that it is based on Amazon's leadership principles and values (Golding, 2017). Certainly, the first and foremost company value is its customer (*"customer obsession"*) when *"leaders start with the customer and work backwards"* (Amazon Jobs, no data).

Besides, the emphasis is laid on such values as the necessity of continuous learning and development, on the ability to make processes better and simpler, and on the ability to see a long-term profit and effectiveness. For the employees to be able to fully exercise their leadership principles related to continuous improvement of the processes, a *"digital employee-suggestion box"* is provided (Green, 2015). Using this service, any employee can submit a suggestion aimed at the improvement of the company's work. Thus, the company showed in practice that it does not simply proclaim leadership slogans but also suggests effective mechanisms for their realization. A perfect example of this policy's success is the suggestion made by Amazon engineer Charlie Ward, through the digital employee-suggestion box (Green, 2015). Its essence was the creation of Amazon Prime, the service of digital paid-for subscription, by means of which customers could receive various allowances and privileges. The customers were rather positive in their attitude to this service. It was recorded that *"on average, Prime members spend about $1,500 a year while non-members spend about $625"* (Kirkham, 2017).

It should be also noted that the company sticks to its requirements of the employees being most customer-centered and observing *"high standards"* by means of the corresponding compensation and benefits policy. For instance, Amazon offers its employees benefits related to health care, employee families' support discounts, discounts on purchases, and financial counseling (The Amazon blog, no data). The average salary for the US fulfillment center workers is $15 per hour, while the federal minimum wages in the United States is only $7.25 (The Amazon blog, no data; Fisman and Luca, 2018). Besides, Amazon increased the minimum salary for UK employees working at equivalent positions: £10.50 an hour in London and £9.50 across the rest of the country, while the minimum salary throughout the country at £8.21 (Partington, 2018; GOV.UK, no data). In India, blue-collar workers of Amazon get 25–60% more than the *"state-mandated minimum wages"* (Variyar, 2018).

However, in some European countries, such as Spain, Germany, and Poland, there were no across-the-board increase of minimum wages; so, the employees expressed their dissatisfaction with their working conditions, which resulted in strikes (Moon, 2018; Prakash, 2019).

It cannot go unmentioned that the company is often subject to criticism, as the working conditions in the company are too harsh. The authors of the most high-profile publication in the *New York Times* wrote that *"at Amazon, workers are encouraged to tear apart one another's ideas in meetings, toil long and late … and held to standards that the company boasts are 'unreasonably high'"* (Kantor and Streitfeld, 2015).

Bezos instantly answered the criticism, emphasizing that *"the article doesn't describe the Amazon I know or the caring Amazonians I work with every day"* (Bezos, 2015). Bezos points out that *"It's not easy to work here – 'You can work long, hard, or smart, but at Amazon.com you can't choose two out of three'"* (Bezos, 1997:4).

Despite the facts presented, according to statistics, the general satisfaction with work in the company is 3.8 out of 5, and the employees gave the highest grade to the Compensation and Benefits program (3.9), while the lowest grade was given to the Work/Life Balance program (3.3) (Glassdoor, 2019).

It was also revealed that 76% of the company personnel would recommend their friends to work in Amazon, 86% approve the activity of the company CEO, and 71% give the company their positive evaluation (Glassdoor, 2019). These numbers testify to the fact that the employees are satisfied with the work in the company than the other way round.

But the presence of objective criticism, a low score in the Work/Life Balance category (3.3), indicates that the company should pay more attention to its employees, who form the basis of customer centricity. Apparently, the company understands this fact and Bezos (2018) notes that investments in staff development and retention will be continued.

Rather a serious attention is paid to the recruitment. The company site describes in detail the process of communication with Amazon for those wishing to be employed (Amazon job, no data). With the first minutes of cooperation with the company, a special stress is laid on its site that any employee is the follower of the company's history, and exceptional customer centricity is the basis for the company's operation. The company explains the features which a future employee must possess, focusing again on customer centricity *"to make smart, fast decisions, stay nimble, innovate and invent and focus on delighting customers"* (Amazon job, no data). It is also remarked that the company does not seek employees meeting *"high standard"*, explaining that *"people are pretty good at learning high standards simply through exposure"* (Bezos, 2017:1). The company policy is initially aimed at future employees' understanding of the company's key requirement, related to customer centricity, and their readiness to learn up to the level of a *"high standard"*.

Amazon also demonstrates the features of systems thinking. As it was already noted, systems thinking is the process in which a system is viewed as a singular entity consisting of various interacting parts (Ackoff, 1999; Jackson, 2003). Owing to continuous integrated interaction of the system's parts, the tasks set are being solved more successfully, which facilitates the system's development and stability (Senge, 2004).

Ackoff (1999) remarks that systematic approach requires the following tactics: for solution to a problem, it is necessary to find the features that unite various sides. It is the main principle and value of Amazon that facilitates the integration of the company's personnel and all its systems, and this is exclusive customer centricity. In other words, the solution of any task in the company must be grounded on considering the customer's interests, which is a starting point for all company's employees.

The example of effective integration in the company could be observed with Amazon Prime, the service of paid-for subscription, offering prompt (one or two days) and free-of-charge delivery (Amazon, no data). Without the corresponding cooperation of the Prime service implementers and the employees who were responsible for the provision of exclusive customer delivery to the Prime subscribers, this service would have been impossible, as it presumes the promptest order delivery to the service subscribers. The Amazon Prime example vividly illustrates another postulate: a change in one company part will essentially lead to changes in all parts of the company, which are interrelated with it. If the introduction of the Prime service hadn't caused corresponding changes in the company's logistics, aimed at the delivery to a customer within two days, the new service would hardly have been possible. Amazon marketing managers' contribution was also necessary as well as the contribution of other employees responsible for the promotion of this service and for customer communication.

For instance, in 2019, the number of Amazon Prime users reached 62% of the total number of Amazon's customers (Clement, 2019). This data presents a clear demonstration of the fact that Amazon Prime is created in the interest of the customers who actively use its advantages.

Senge (2004) notes that systems thinking can bring about a union of physical and social sciences, engineering, and management for the solution of the tasks set, which is demonstrated by Amazon. David Zapolsky, Senior Vice President, General Counsel, and Secretary, emphasizes that the company's culture impels the lawyers to take part in the CX discussions, irrespective of whether there is any current legal problem and this gives a persistent positive feeling of a contribution to the common cause (Alexander, 2017). Bezos states that employees frequently approach him with their new tasks, and together they find an optimal solution, which is later carried to perfection by other company employees (Bloomberg Markets and Finance, 2018).

Thus, Amazon, consolidated by common principles and value, presents a vivid example of systems interaction.

In sum, this analysis of Amazon showed that the company leader Jeff Bezos is a true protagonist of a customer-centered approach to doing business. This approach is fully shared by the Amazon's top management and supported by its personnel. In the company, a customer-centered culture, vision, and values exist, which help the employees in creating and executing an effective CX. In the example of Amazon Prime service, based on the observations of the company's leader and top management, it is possible to state that the personnel are systematically interacting with the purpose of creating the best value proposition for the company's customers. Amazon also makes maximum efforts to develop customer centricity and necessary professional skills with the personnel. Besides, due attention is paid in the company to the personnel's motivation.

It should also be stated that, in general, Amazon's work with its personnel brings positive results, and the personnel demonstrate the necessary customer centricity rate. Otherwise, the company brand would not have taken the third place with the potential capacity for further growth in the list of 100 brands (Interbrand, 2019). What especially stands out is the ability of Amazon to most fully satisfy its customers' requirements.

It can be confirmed that Amazon personnel is the basis of CX and they actively participate in its execution and improvement.

Integrated Marketing

Key Points
- Existence of integrated customer communication channels grounded on the common idea
- Information suitability to the target audience requirements

- Personalized suggestions to customers
- Planning integrated marketing communications and measuring of their effectiveness.

Goal
- Creation of value-consolidated proposition for the customers by means of integrated communication channels.

A demonstrative example of integrated marketing in Amazon was presented by the advertising campaign of the Amazon Prime Day, a global shopping event, which started on July 15, 2015, lasted for 24 hours, and was offered in nine countries (The Amazon blog, 2019). This action was aimed at demonstrating the advantages of the paid-for Prime service, which presupposes various bonuses and prompt free-of-charge delivery for its subscribers.

While the event was in progress, the service subscribers could purchase via Amazon various goods and services at rather attractive prices. In addition, this action was bound to the company's birthday (The Amazon blog, 2019). To advertise this action, nine days before the start of the Amazon Prime Day, the company sent personal e-mails to potential customers, the frequency of opening them being 41% (Harris, 2016). Besides, the described action was supported in social networks and traditional media (Harris, 2016).

The action quite met the customers' expectations of cooperation with Amazon, which, according to Bezos (1998:2), find their expression in *"ease-of-use, low prices, and service that we deliver"*.

Amazon also conducted the measurements of the action (The Amazon blog, 2019):

- The amount of sold goods was bigger than that on "Black Friday" of 2014.
- The sales grew 300%.
- 34.4 million goods were ordered.
- The sales of Amazon devices demonstrated a considerable growth.

So, judging by the facts, this carefully planned action is a classic example of integrated marketing communications when all marketing activities were united by one aim, complementing each other. The sense of the action correlated with the customers' expectations from communication with the company.

Amazon also uses integrated marketing communication for its various seasonal activities. For instance, all its social channels – Facebook (no data), Twitter (no data), and YouTube (no data) – were united with one slogan, unique in its design, reminding of the beginning of a school year: *"Happy School Year"*.

On the example of the action, devoted to the advertisement of the Amazon Prime service, one can see that Amazon actively uses integrated marketing communications to interact with the customers. The company plans the creation of integrated marketing communication with consideration of the customers' requirements and the mandatory assessment of its effectiveness. Judging by successful results of Amazon Prime Day action, integrated marketing is quite an effective CX element. Its correct application helps in creating a consolidated value proposition for the customers, which produces the most positive influence on the sales volume.

Amazon (2018:26) emphasizes that they constantly use the complex approach to engaging in customer communications *"through a number of targeted online marketing channels, such as our sponsored search, third party customer referrals, social and online advertising, television advertising, and other initiatives"*. It is necessary to say that Amazon is one of the biggest advertisers. In 2018 the company spent about $4.47 billion on advertising (Luce, 2019).

Product or Service Marketing

Key Point
- Product or service, meeting the customer's requirements or exceeding them.

Goal
- Creation of customer value proposition by means of the product or service.

It is necessary to note that Amazon's sales is executed by *"independent third party sellers – mostly small- and medium-sized businesses"*, which exercise over 58% of the total sales amount (Bezos, 2018:1). The rest is made directly by goods and services of Amazon. The company offers its customers its own goods and services, such as home security products, the e-book reading device Kindle, Amazon videos, and so on (Amazon, no data). Amazon Kindle takes the leading position in ratings and is one of the best e-book reading devices (Colon, 2020). Owing to such an approach, Amazon's customers have permanent access to the most comprehensive range of goods and services, consisting of 33 groups, which include handmade foods, health goods, and other categories (Amazon Services, no data).

The company makes maximum efforts for the goods or services to be safe for the customers. For instance, concerning the category *"Luggage & Travel Accessories"*, Amazon points out that *"we do not allow any counterfeit, replica, or knock-off products"* (Amazon Services, no data).

Corson, director, Amazon North America Customer Fulfillment, Environmental Health and Safety, notes: *"When we think about being the most customer-centric organization, we (also) want to be the most safety-centric organization in the world"* (Garnet, 2019). It is safety that is the basic requirement of any person and one of the key requirements for the quality of any product or service (Maslow, 1970; Stevenson, 2015).

Special attention should be given to the Amazon e-commerce platform, which is used to engage in communications of the *"customer–company"* type. As the foregoing analysis shows, Amazon.com's e-commerce platform has the following features:

- Understandable enough to communicate with the customers;
- Provides a friendly and convenient interface;
- Accessible for customers continuously and without a break;
- Offers recommendations for optimal engineering of mutually beneficial cooperation;
- Develops constantly, with more and more usage of artificial intelligence for creating personalized customer propositions (CNBC, 2019).

Bezos states that Amazon is *"working to build a place where customers can find and discover anything they want to buy, anytime, anywhere"* (Bezos, 1999:3).

It is emphasized that the company continuously analyses its product suite, works at the reduction of delivery terms, pays attention to its price policy and product safety, analyzes the customers' opinions (Bezos, letters 1997–2018). There exist all grounds to assume that Amazon continuously works at maintaining its products' *"acceptability, affordability, accessibility, and awareness"*.

It is also necessary to pay attention to the fact that Amazon strives for exceeding their customers' expectations. For instance, the company is *"working toward offering One-Day Delivery"* instead of two-day delivery, announced earlier, for the Prime service subscribers (Amazon, 2019). Bezos (1998:3) underlines that *"the company intends to build out a significant distribution infrastructure to meet all customers' demands in the best way"*.

So, owing to a well-chosen approach to offering products to the customers and a convenient service, Amazon managed to create a real value proposition. Choosing from a huge variety of goods or services, potential customers can see that these goods and services underwent the necessary selection and meet the quality requirements, as required by Amazon.

The success of the accomplished proposition is also supported, more specifically, by the following fact: if in March 2016 the number of the Amazon Prime (the paid-for subscription service) customers was 58 million active users, then already in June 2019 it went up to about 105 million (Clement, 2019). Consequently, the customers demonstrate their positive evaluation of the goods offered by Amazon as well as of the company's service.

Relationship Marketing

Key Points
• Existing effective bonds with clients and other stakeholders

Goals
• Provision of continuous engagement development of the personnel into CX creation and realization.

First of all, it should be noted that the company determines its stakeholders and evaluates the communication level with them independently (Berry, 1995). On the basis of the information obtained by means of analyzing Bezos' letters to shareholders (letters 1997–2018), Amazon's annual reports (1997–2018), and Amazon's site in the Internet – Amazon.com, the following company's stakeholders were selected for detailed consideration:

• Customers
• Employees
• Third-party sellers
• Suppliers
• Community
• Shareholders

Customers

According to Bezos (1997), it is thanks to the customers that Amazon has the opportunity to generate profit and assure its further development. Customers also demonstrate their interest in cooperating with the company. This is manifested by the fact that the number of purchases of the paid-for service Prime subscribers grows both in the United States and in all countries where Amazon is operating. If in 2016 net sales, from this service's customers, was $6.394 billion, already in 2018 this increased to $14.168 billion (Amazon, 2018).

As it was mentioned above, Amazon utilizes its customer communications rather effectively by means of integrated marketing communications. Besides, the company created a unique product and service proposition, which received high evaluation by its customers.

It is evident that the company and its customers generate the value, necessary for both: the company offers its customers qualitative goods and services, while the customers generate profit.

According to the research data, 48% consumers of Amazon visit the online platform several times a week and 89% at least once a month (Feedvisor, 2019). It is also stated that 96% of the Prime subscribers renew their membership after their two-year usage of this service (CIRP, 2016).

Thus, by the unique proposition of embracing the variety of the presented product or service and effective communications, the company established long-term relationships with its customers.

Bezos (1999:3) notes that the company will continuously strive for *"growing and strengthening customer relationships"*. For instance, with the help of the Prime Video service, Amazon *"continues to drive Prime member adoption and retention"* (Bezos, 2017:4).

By opening a physical store, Amazon offered its existing and potential customers the option to become familiar with and buy the most top-rated goods that can be purchased on its e-commerce platform (Amazon, no data). Doing this, the company certainly facilitated the creation of closer bonds with the customers who can now become familiar with the goods and buy them in a real shop as well as online. Such approach received the name of research online purchase offline (ROPO), or vice versa, when the customers can choose between offline and online channels (Binder, 2014).

It is emphasized that Amazon will continuously *"retain and increase sales to existing customers, attract new customers, and satisfy our customers' demands"* (Amazon, 2017:6).

Employees

Bezos (1997:5) states that Amazon's success depends on the company's *"ability to attract and retain a motivated employee base"*. Such attention to the personnel is conditioned by the fact that it is the personnel who create and implement the company's CX and generate the value for the customers and other stakeholders. It is noted that the level of CX quality is in direct relation to the employees' ability to cooperate with the customers, to propose the necessary service to them, and to demonstrate the company's friendly attitude (Yohn, 2018).

So, the employees are the key players in the creation of CX, with whom the company must establish the closest bonds and communications. A vivid example of personnel communications is the Connection Program, the Amazon initiative aimed at continuous interaction with the personnel(Kim, 2018). The core of the program is that employees give daily answers to the question related to their work and organization of labor. These answers are later analyzed by the managers for necessary decisions to be made, which could facilitate positive changes in the current situation.

Thus, the employees see that their voice is not simply heard, the company also takes necessary steps to realize the expressed suggestions. Owing to the Connection Program, Amazon strives to expand the employees' engagement into the processes that are happening in the company.

As it was already mentioned, the greatest contribution into the CX development is made by the engaged personnel, who do not simply share customer-centered values and follow them but invest maximum efforts to realize these values (Vance, 2006). Broadening of the employees' engagement requires constant bilateral communications between the company and its personnel.

As Kopp (2019) noted, the most effective method to measure the employees' engagement rate is a survey. Because within this study framework conducting a survey turns to be impossible, the conditions in Amazon will be analyzed, because of which the employees are engaged into the process of positive customer CX creation.

These conditions include the following:

1   The employees' self-motivation for creating the best CX and suggesting it to the customer.

ouchenour and Chrisman (2016) state that self-motivation is the process in which a person understands his or her ability of independent influence on the situation and of taking necessary actions without any impact on other people and circumstances. According to Geller and Veazie (2017), a self-motivated person must be sure that the actions he or she is going to perform are necessary and these efforts will help in achieving the target goals, which are sure to fetch the desirable results.

Therefore, to develop the employees' self-motivation, the following conditions must be created in the company:

1   Encouragement of independence in decision taking.
2   Employees must be sure that their activities in the company will do good for them.

It should be stated that in Amazon the emphasis is made on the employees' maximum independence in taking decisions and observing high standards of work even if *"no one is watching"* (Bezos, 2017:3). The Worldwide Consumer CEO Jeff Wilke underlines that the company greatly appreciates such features as the ability to think and act from the owner position, addiction to customer centricity, and continuous development (McCracken, 2019). Besides, the employees can see that the company's success in the sphere of positive customer relationships development has an impact on their financial well-being.

The data of Glassdoor (no data) shows that the point *"Compensation and Benefits"* scores 3.9 out of 5, which is not a bad index at all. Thus, the employees understand that customer-centered behavior and independence in decision taking are expected from them, and that such behavior is beneficial both for themselves and the company. Judging from this information, it can be stated that in Amazon there exist necessary conditions that help the employees in being self-motivated for the achievement of the high-ranking CX.

2   Support of employees in following the "customer first" principle.

In Amazon, there exists the Virtual Customer Service team, the main target of which is delivering timely, accurate, and professional customer service to Amazon customers, helping solve their problems (Amazon jobs, no data). This program makes provisions for the employees to assist the customers while being in comfortable home surroundings. This example demonstrates that the company exercises all-round support to the personnel in realizing the principle "Obsessing over customers".

3   Existence of the necessary technical basis to create and exercise the effective CX.

The company possesses the *"Amazon Customer Service Technology"*, which continuously develops products for CX improvement. The main purpose of this service is automatic performance promotion, aimed not only at the convenience of customer–company cooperation but also at developing decisions that help the employees improve cooperation with the customers (Amazon Jobs, no data).

These three mentioned factors being present enable presuming that the company uses maximum efforts to create effective bonds with its employees and to engage them into CX creation and implementation. It is noted that the more engaged employees the company has, the higher its CX is (Yohn, 2018).

Third-Party Sellers

All the importance of third-party sellers (independent sellers offering goods or services on the e-commerce platform) for Amazon can be illustrated with the following fact: the Annual Report-2018 (p. 1) starts with the statistics on this segment, stating that between 1999 and 2018 *"Third-party sales have grown from 3% of the total to 58%."* This part of the report also includes the data in money terms: *"third-party sales have grown from $0.1 billion to $160 billion"* (Amazon, 2018:1). Considering the facts presented, one clear-cut conclusion can be made that third-party sellers produce a considerable impact on the Amazon CX. In the company, it is noted that *"third-party sales have become a successful and significant part"* (Amazon, 2005). It is also emphasized that Amazon will use all efforts to make the cooperation for this stakeholder most understandable and convenient (Amazon, 2018). In order to improve the cooperation with third-party sellers, Amazon has spent *"tens of billions"* of US dollars since 2011 (Wilke, 2019).

The formula for cooperation with third-party sellers is very simple: *"You sell it, we ship it"* (Amazon services, no data). In the relevant chapter, Amazon introduces a detailed explanation for potential customers as to how to build their relationships with third-party sellers (Amazon, no data).

Amazon emphasizes that one of the key factors, influencing its success, is their *"ability to retain and expand our network of sellers"* (Amazon, 2018:6). As the company states, 4000 purchases a minute are made on its platform particularly by independent sellers (Amazon, 2019).

So, the given figures and facts show that Amazon uses quite a lot of efforts to create and develop an effective marketing network, consisting of third-party sellers.

Suppliers

As concerns suppliers, it is necessary to say that unlike Tesco and Samsung, Amazon has no *"long-term arrangements"* with the majority of its suppliers (Amazon, 2018:13; Samsung, 2017; Tesco, 2017).

Nevertheless, it is emphasized in Amazon that supplier relationships are extremely important because the success of the whole work depends on the cooperation with this stakeholder (Bezos, 1999:4). Besides, the company understands that if *"suppliers violate applicable laws"*, the requirements of ethics or environmental safety and compliance, it can have a negative effect on Amazon's reputation, operating results, and further development (Amazon, 2018:13).

That is why, to create productive relationships with suppliers, Amazon attaches the highest importance to its cooperation with them:

1   In Amazon, the *"Supply Chain Standards Manual"* was worked out, which *"provides guidance for suppliers to ensure that their practices meet and exceed the expectations in Amazon's Supplier Code of Conduct"* (Amazon, no data).
2   Training for suppliers are conducted, aimed at the performance of necessary standards (Amazon, no data);
3   Regular assessment of the suppliers' activity is conducted (Amazon, no data).

Amazon underlines that it may *"terminate its relationships at any time"* with any supplier, which violates Supplier Code and if it does not co-operate during assessments (Amazon, no data). At the same time, it is stated that Amazon is ready for the closest cooperation with suppliers who observe the provisions of the "Supplier Code of Conduct".

It should be noted that according to the signal theory provisions (Connelly et al., 2011), by cooperating with the Amazon brand, suppliers send a signal on their reliability, which will be positively taken by potential and existing partners. For its part, Amazon, with due respect for its suppliers, receives a guarantee of unfailing provision with necessary goods and services. Thus, both the company and its suppliers create for each other mutual value expressed in mutually beneficial cooperation.

Community

In Amazon, attention is also paid to the interaction with society and local communities, the members of which are highly probable potential or real customers of the company. For instance, in India Amazon is *"empowering young minds through education & skilling"* through the "Innovative Science Labs" and "Evening Tuition Centre" (Parekh, 2018).

In Germany, Amazon cooperates with the company supplying meals for students, and this cooperation *"converted more than 16,000 breakfasts for schoolchildren"* (The Amazon blog, no data). Through collaboration with the organization called World Reader, Amazon *"is donating thousands of Kindle digital readers to support reading programs in developing countries"* (Amazon.com.br, no data). Local communities of the United States also receive support from the company. In particular, there exist assistance programs for people having difficulties with dwelling (The Amazon blog, 2020).

Amazon also pays a very close attention to the protection of nature, working at limiting carbon shipment and creating alternative pollutant-free energy sources (The Amazon blog, 2020). Moreover, Bezos has committed $10 billion to combat climate change (Schleifer, 2020).

Actions of such kind are philanthropic in character. They are considered to be part of a social agreement between business and society (Archie and Buchholtz, 2009). According to Nielsen (2014) research, most customers have a more favorable attitude for companies demonstrating their social responsibility.

Shareholders

Special attention in Amazon is given to relationships with investors and shareholders. The site Amazon.com contains a separate chapter called *"Investors Relationship"* where one can find the necessary information on the company's financial results and annual reports. There also exist the form of feedback and document requests for shareholders. It is important to say that Bezos as Amazon's CEO informs the company shareholders on the results obtained and the company development plans by means of his letters, submitted on an annual basis (Bezos, letters 1997–2018).

Clearly Amazon is sure that *"the long-term interests of shareholders are tightly linked to the interests of our customers"* (Bezos, 2001:3). It is emphasized that effective relationships with the customers and a continuous growth of their number produce the most positive impact on the company's profit, generating more long-term value for shareholders (The Amazon blog, no data).

According to Archie and Buchholtz (2009:142), relations with shareholders can be quite difficult for the company, as they *"group with a range of interests and expectations"* and therefore can influence the company's development. However, it is emphasized in Amazon that they have support from their shareholders (The Amazon blog, no data).

Thus, Amazon and its shareholders generate mutual value for each other: shareholders provide support that the company needs and approve its strategy, while the company demonstrates steady development and effective financial results. Amazon notes that the company is thankful to its shareholders *"for your support, your encouragement, and for joining us on this adventure"* (The Amazon blog, no data).

To conclude, the example with Amazon showed that mutually beneficial relationships not only with the customers but with the rest of stakeholders are rather a high priority for the company. Quite much attention is given to building marketing networks with the stakeholders for facilitating effective bilateral communications. Besides, the necessary conditions are created in Amazon for the personnel's engagement into CX creation and execution.

Performance Marketing

Key Points
- CX planning, CX execution and monitoring, CX assessment.

Goal
- CX continuous development and upgrading.

The analysis of Amazon's Annual Reports and Jeff Bezos' letters in the period 1997–2018 showed that Amazon's development is built on planning, with due consideration of the customers' requirements. In the company, it is stated that *"It's critical to ask customers what they want, listen carefully to their answers, and figure out a plan to provide it thoughtfully and quickly (speed matters in business!)"* (Bezos, 2018:2).

For instance, in 1998 the company aimed to build value for the customer, expand the customer base, and strengthen the brand (Bezos, 1998). To achieve these goals, continuous investments were planned as well as creating the company–customer cooperation system, most convenient for the customers.

Amazon's goal for 1999 was creating a company with a multibillion profit, which could serve its customers *"with operational excellence and high efficiency"* (Bezos, 1998). In 2000 Amazon planned *"growing and strengthening customer relationships"*, continuous CX improvement, and making investments into new customer acquisition (Bezos, 2000).

It is noted in the company that they exercise regular control over the goal achievement process, with necessary corrections when needed. They emphasize that the majority of their aims are related to the improvement of customer cooperation.

To create the best customer experience, Amazon follows two strategies: cost leadership and differentiation, which determine all planning of CX development. The strategy of cost leadership presupposes obtaining competitive advantage by offering the most attractive prices (Porter, 1990). The company states that they stick to two extremely important approaches: continuous work at the price policy and simultaneous offer of the most qualitative service. It is said that attractive prices specifically facilitate the creation of the best CX, which finally *"will produce more value for shareholders"* (Bezos, 2003).

As for the strategy of differentiation, it presupposes that goods or services, offered by the company, are more attractive than those of their competitors and can be associated with functionality, durability, the company's support, and the brand image (Porter, 1990). They note in Amazon that the basis of their differentiation is *"constant innovation and relentless focus on customer"* (Bezos, 1998:3). This approach is the cornerstone of Amazon's competitive advantage.

Consequently, CX creation and development will be focused on offering competitive prices, innovations, and maximum satisfaction of customers' requirements. Moreover, Amazon pays attention to giving assessment to the effectiveness of its activities. With this aim, the company keeps a sharp focus on such indices as "sales growth", "cumulative customer accounts", "the percentage of orders from repeat customers", and "audience reach, per media metrics" (Bezos, 1997).

The company is always attentive to the fact that measuring the effectiveness of their activities is extremely important for the company's development, as it allows a critical evaluation both of successes and failures, and consequently, to create a more effective development program.

At the same time, the people in Amazon prefer concentrating not only on indices evaluating the present-moment success but on how well the company managed to provide the *"creation of long-term value"* (Amazon, 2019:42). For instance, they are sure that the best success indicator is the *"stock price performance over the long term"* (Amazon, 2019:43).

Further, emphasis is placed on the importance of monitoring the process of achievement of targets, and the success of investments made reflecting in the resulting performance. Bezos (2014:2) notes that considerable sums were invested into the development of the Prime Instant Video service; that is why *"it's important that we monitor its impact"*. The monitoring results show this project's success, so the investments will be continued.

The data on the growth of third-party sellers, suggesting their goods or services on the company's platform, enable Amazon making the conclusion of a successful cooperation with the given stakeholder (Amazon, 2018). So, Amazon keeps a close watch on the satisfaction of its top important stakeholder, belonging to a 'non-customer' group.

Thus, enough attention is given in Amazon to planning, execution, and monitoring, and effectiveness of execution and the evaluation of their actions. Besides, the analysis showed that planning of the company's activity is done on the basis of *"cost leadership"* and *"differentiation"* strategies.

It is emphasized in the company that such an approach, under which development is built on the basis of the customers' requirements, planning, and evaluation of the obtained results, is extremely important for the creation of a top-value proposition.

Conclusions

The empirical verification of CX model (CXM) using the example of Amazon provided the following results:

1   *Internal marketing.* Customer-centered leader and personnel and their cooperation are the main source of effective CX creation. The key role in customer centricity development is played by the vision of the company development, its values, and culture. The closest attention is also paid to the personnel's continuous development and corresponding motivation. In Amazon, the conditions are created for the personnel's direct participation in CX creation and development.

2   *Integrated marketing.* Due to effective integrated marketing communications, the company creates the customer value proposition, which with time produces a positive influence on its financial well-being. Integrated marketing communications may have the character of both general and personalized customer propositions. Attention is given to planning and to the evaluation of the effectiveness of integrated marketing communication outcomes.

3   *Product/service marketing.* Amazon's products or services form the basis of the company's value proposition. The company tries to completely satisfy or surpass the customers' requirements.

4   *Relationship marketing.* Constant productive relationships with customers and key stakeholders help the company in creating

marketing networks, which has a positive impact on its client centricity rate. In Amazon, the importance of both customer acquisition and customer retention is emphasized.

5 *Performance marketing.* In Amazon, due attention is paid to planning, to effectiveness assessment, and monitoring of actions performed, which allows to constantly improve customer cooperation.

It can be placed on record that all key points, inherent to each CXM elements, are not simply present in the company but actively facilitate CX creation and development. Thus, the suggested model of CX creation passed its empirical verification and can be used for creation of unique customer experience.

The analysis also showed that all elements of the model are meaningful for CX execution and creation. However, without a customer-centered leader and personnel, the creation and formation of a customer-centered company appears to be impossible. Consequently, this element forms the basis for the formation of customer centricity and CX.

It is necessary to underline that at the very beginning of its existence, Amazon has been persistently following its top important principle of "customer first". This approach allows the company to achieve exceptional financial results. As it can be seen in Figure 5.1, from 1995 to 2018, Amazon has been constantly demonstrating the upward trend of the net sales index; it testifies to the constant growth of customer activity.

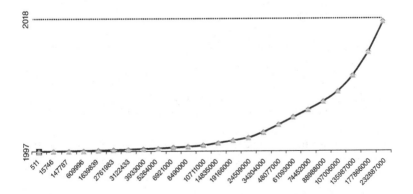

Figure 5.1 Amazon net sales index 1995–2018 (in million US dollars).
Source of data: Amazon annual reports 1997–2018.

6 Concluding Remarks

In the course of this research, its main aim has been accomplished, namely, the creation of the model of effective customer experience formation (CXM) and the best possible concept of forming a customer-centric company has been suggested. The creation of the model was achieved due to consistent realization of the objectives of this study:

1 Marketing concepts such as marketing myopia, direct marketing, relationship marketing, and holistic marketing were analyzed.
2 On the basis of the conducted analysis, the holistic marketing concept was selected for further consideration, which contained valuable solutions from the previously considered concepts and presuming holistic approach to CX creation.
3 Furthermore, a detailed critical analysis of holistic marketing was performed with the help of theoretical postulates and empirical verification using practical examples from the activity of leading global companies. As a result of this analysis, the CXM as a new marketing concept was worked out, suggesting an optimal approach to the creation of a customer-centered company and the development of CX.
4 Then the suggested model was empirically verified using the example of Amazon, the technology company that proclaims customer centricity to be the foundation of its business.

While conducting the research, relevant academic and business literature was referred, and reliable sources of documentary information, such as annual reports of companies, research data, and statistics, were used.

Finally, a reliable and verified tool – the customer experience model (CXM) – was proposed, the use of which will allow a company to meet or to exceed customers' expectations in the best possible way. Then, in the course of research, the hypothesis that the leader and the company's personnel and their cooperation is the basis of customer centricity was confirmed without doubt. Consequently, while creating a customer-centered company, closest attention should be given to the personnel's development and to their ability to meet and anticipate the customers' requirements in the best way. A convincing proof of the idea that it is the leaders and CEOs who are the "starting point" in creating an effective customer experience and customer centricity was established.

In the research, the exceptional importance of orientation on customer's requirements for the company's successful development was shown. The emphasis was placed on the need for the application of systems thinking, on the implementation of the learning organization principles, and on the use of "Lewinian experiential learning cycle" for effective CX formation and development.

Attention should also be paid to the fact that learning organization and systems thinking are the key factors for the creation of complex adaptive systems (Senge, 2004). Complex adaptive systems (CAS) presuppose the existence of cooperating and interrelated agents, determining the development of the whole system (Chan, 2001; Gell-Mann, 1994).

The following are the advantages of CAS (Chan, 2001; Gell-Mann, 1994; Lichtenstein et al., 2006):

1   Absence of a rigid control system;
2   Capacity for independent adaptation to changing conditions;
3   Capacity for self-development.

It is possible to assume that the transformation of customer centricity into CAS will help companies to obtain a self-regulating system, capable of further development, aimed at the best satisfaction of customers' requirements. Thus, the attitude to customer centricity in CAS will be the topic for a new study.

As it was already observed, the main customer centricity requirement is the need for hearing the customer's voice and acting in accordance with his or her wishes. However, the following questions arise: to which degree the company must respond to all customers' requirements, what is the optimal way of building a dialogue between a company and its customers, and where should a company pay attention to for the purpose of building most effective long-term relations. These issues require a more detailed study, as the company's further development and success depend on the level of its cooperation with its customers.

The subject of additional research is the issue of a company's co-operation with its stakeholders and their influence on the compa-ny's relationships with its customers. Thus, this research mapped out the tasks, the decisions of which will facilitate more effective satisfaction of the customers' requirements.

In conclusion, the emphasis should be placed on the fact that cus-tomer experience is simultaneously *"art and science"* (Conder et al., 2014; Savitz, 2011). The suggested model demonstrates the main benchmarks of CX creation, structuring the process. However, the experience resulting from CX creation and new knowledge open limitless opportunities to companies for the advancement of this model and for the search of one's own unique path to collaborate with customers.

References

Abodaher, David (1985), *Lee Iacocca*, New York, NY: Zebra Books.

Ackoff, Russel (1999), "A Lifetime of System Thinking", *Pegasus Communications* Vol. 10, No. 5, available at https://thesystemsthinker.com/wp-content/uploads/pdfs/100501pk.pdf (accessed 16 February 2020).

Ackoff, Russel; Addison, Herbert and Carey, Andrew (2010), *Systems Thinking for Curious Managers*, Charmouth: Triarchy Press.

Adidas (2012), "Adidas Group at a Glance 2012", available at www.adidas-group.com/media/filer_public/2013/07/31/adidas_gb_2012_en_booklet_en.pdf (accessed 20 October 2019).

Adidas (2013), "Annual Report 2013", available at www.adidas-group.com/media/filer_public/2014/03/05/adidas-group_gb_2013_en.pdf (accessed 4 February 2020).

Adidas (2015), "Annual Report 2015", available at www.adidas-group.com/media/filer_public/e9/73/e973acf3-f889-43e5-b3c0-bc870d53b964/2015_gb_en.pdf (accessed 4 February 2020).

Adidas (2016), "Annual Report 2016", available at www.adidas-group.com/media/filer_public/a3/fb/a3fb7068-c556-4a24-8eea-cc00951a1061/2016_eng_gb.pdf (accessed 9 February 2020).

Adidas (2017), "Annual Report 2017", available at www.adidas-group.com/media/filer_public/6a/69/6a690baa-8430-42c5-841d-d9222a150aff/annual_report_gb-2017_en_secured.pdf (accessed 20 October 2019).

Adidas (2018), "Annual Report 2018", available at https://report.adidas-group.com/fileadmin/user_upload/adidas_Annual_Report_GB-2018-EN.pdf (accessed 20 October 2019).

Alexander, Tiffani (2017), "Q&A with the EiC: Managing Global Risks with Amazon GC David Zapolsky", available at www.accdocket.com/articles/q-a-with-eic-global-risks-amazon-gc-david-zapolsky.cfm (accessed 20 October 2019).

Alsadeq, Imad and Hakam, Tarek (2010), [Project Management Institute], Meet the New Project Manager – Mr. KPI. Paper presented at PMI® Global Congress 2010–EMEA, Milan, Italy. Newtown Square, available at www.pmi.org/learning/library/project-managers-strategic-objectives-value-6827 (accessed 31 January 2020).

Amazon (no data), "About Ordering from a Third-Party Seller", available at www.amazon.com/gp/help/customer/display.html?nodeId=201889310 (accessed 4 March 2019).

Amazon (no data), "Amazon Devices", available at www.amazon.com/amazon-devices/b?ie=UTF8&node=2102313011&ref_=footer_devices (accessed 19 February 2020).

Amazon (no data), "Amazon 4 Star Westfield Topanga", available at www.amazon.com/amazon-4-star/b/?node=17988552011 (accessed 1 March 2020).

Amazon (no data), "Amazon Supply Chain Standards", available at https://d39w7f4ix9f5s9.cloudfront.net/de/48/a468a0be42da83d58b72019bb1c7/amazon-supply-chain-standards-2019.pdf (accessed 5 March 2020).

Amazon (no data), "Supply Chain Standards Manual", available at https://d39w7f4ix9f5s9.cloudfront.net/ba/73/23a785f24c809ee05445d5ab623f/supplier-manual-5sep2019-final.pdf (accessed 5 March 2020).

Amazon (2016), "Investor Relationship", available at https://ir.about amazon.com/static-files/0f9e36b1-7e1e-4b52-be17-145dc9d8b5ec (accessed 23 October 2019).

Amazon (2017), "Annual Report", available at https://ir.aboutamazon.com/static-files/917130c5-e6bf-4790-a7bc-cc43ac7fb30a (accessed 14 February 2020).

Amazon (2018), "Annual Report", available at https://ir.aboutamazon.com/static-files/0f9e36b1-7e1e-4b52-be17-145dc9d8b5ec (accessed 14 February 2020).

Amazon (1997–2018), "Annual Reports", available at https://ir.aboutamazon.com/annual-reports (accessed 29 February 2020).

Amazon (2019a), "Amazon SMB Impact Report", available at https://d39w7f4ix9f5s9.cloudfront.net/61/3b/1f0c2cd24f37bd0e3794c284cd-2f/2019-amazon-smb-impact-report.pdf (accessed 4 March 2020).

Amazon (2019b), "Notice of 2019 Annual Meeting of Shareholders", available at https://ir.aboutamazon.com/static-files/35fa4e12-78bd-40bc-a700-59eea3dbd23b (accessed 5 March 2020).

Amazon (2019c), "Prime Delivery Benefits You May Not Know About", available at www.amazon.com/primeinsider/tips/all-pr-delivery-benefits.html (accessed 20 February 2020).

Amazon Job (no data), "6 Things You Should Know about Prime Delivery", available at www.amazon.com/primeinsider/tips/prime-delivery-faq.html (accessed 15 February 2020).

Amazon Job (no data), "About Amazon", available at www.amazon.jobs/en-gb/landing_pages/about-amazon (accessed 15 February 2020).

Amazon Jobs (no data), "Customer Service Technology", available at www.amazon.jobs/en/teams/customer-service-technology (accessed 1 March 2020).

Amazon Jobs (no data), "Earth's Most Customer-Centric Company", available at www.amazon.jobs/en/working/working-amazon (accessed 15 February 2020).

Amazon Jobs (no data), "Obsessing over Customers", available at www.amazon.jobs/en/teams/customer-service-associates (accessed 1 March 2020).

Amazon News (2018), [YouTube], Q&A with Jeff Wilke, CEO of Worldwide Consumer at Amazon, available at www.youtube.com/watch?v=RqlvSuZMIyE (accessed 15 February 2020).

Amazon Services (no data), "Amazon Business", available at https://services.amazon.com/amazon-business.html?ld=usb2bunifooter (accessed 4 March 2020).

Amazon Services (no data), "Start Selling Online", available at https://services.amazon.com/services/soa-approval-category.html (accessed 19 February 2020).

Amazon.com.br (no data), "Kindle. Fundo de Leitura Kindle", available at www.amazon.com.br/b?ie=UTF8&node=16593314011&ref_=footer_community (accessed 5 March 2020).

American Express (2017), "Consumer Cards&Services", available at https://about.americanexpress.com/press-release/wellactually-americans-say-customer-service-better-ever (accessed 28 November 2019).

AMZ Begin (no data), "Congratulations to Power Woman Shelley Reynolds", available at www.amzbegin.com/Congratulations-to-Power-Woman-Shelley/blog/62wvb5w5qdgd4sm/ (accessed 15 February 2020).

Anderson, Eugen; Fornell, Claes and Rust, Ronald (1997), "Customer Satisfaction, Productivity, and Profitability: Differences between Goods and Services", *Marketing Science* Vol. 16, No. 2, pp. 129–145. http://bear.warrington.ufl.edu/centers/mks/articles/customersatisfaction.pdf (accessed 16 January 2020).

Anderson, James and Narus, James (1998), [Harvard Business Review], "Business Marketing: Understand What Customers Value", available at https://hbr.org/1998/11/business-marketing-understand-what-customers-value (accessed 29 January 2020).

Andersen, Poul (2011), "Relationship Development and Marketing Communication: An Integrative Model", *Journal of Business & Industrial Marketing* Vol. 16, No. 3, pp. 167–180.

Ang, Lawrence and Buttle, Francis (2010), "Managing for Successful Customer Acquisition: An Exploration", *Journal of Marketing Management* Vol. 22, No. 3–4, pp. 295–317, available at www.tandfonline.com/doi/abs/10.1362/026725706776861217 (accessed 16 January 2020).

Ansoff, H. Igor (2007), *Strategic Management*, New York, NY: Palgrave Macmillan.

Apple, INC (2018), "Form 10-K For the Fiscal Year Ended September 29, 2018", available at www.annualreports.com/HostedData/AnnualReports/PDF/NASDAQ_AAPL_2018.pdf#targetText=The%20Company%20is%20committed%20to, innovative%20hardware%2C%20software%20and%20services.&targetText=The%20Company%20also%20supports%20a, that%20complement%20the%20Company's%20offerings (accessed 30 January 2020).

Atherton, Matt (2017), [Food Manufacture], "Tesco's Organic Sales Climb 15%", available at www.foodmanufacture.co.uk/Article/2017/02/20/ Tesco-organic-food-sales-rise-15 (accessed 17 January 2020).

Baer, Jay (2016), *Hug Your Haters: How to Embrace Complaints and Keep Your Customers*, New York: Penguin Random House, LLC.

Baker, Hughes (2017), "A Holistic Driving Better Outcomes", available at www.industrial.ai/sites/g/files/cozyhq596/files/acquiadam_assets/ bently_nevada_condition_monitoring_product_line.pdf (accessed 3 January 2017).

Bartley, Bronwen; Gomibuchi, Seishi and Mann, Robin (2007), "Best Practices in Achieving a Customer-Focused Culture", *Benchmarking: An International Journal* Vol. 14, No. 4, pp. 482–496.

Bass, Bernard (1990), "From Transactional to Transformational Leadership: Learning to Share the Vision", *Organizational Dynamics* Vol. 18, No. 3, Winter, pp. 19–31.

Bassot, Barbara (2016), *The Reflective Journal*, 2nd edition, London: Palgrave.

BBC (2017), "Samsung Confirms Battery Faults as Cause of Note 7 Fires", available at www.bbc.com/news/business-38714461 (accessed 5 January 2020).

Bemorehuman (2019), "Run Ukraine", available at https://bemorehuman. org.ua/ (accessed 4 December 2020).

Bennis, Warren (2003), *On Becoming a Leader*, New York, NY: Basic Books.

Berry, Leonard (1995), "Relationship Marketing of Services-Growing Interest, Emerging Perspectives", *Journal of the Academy of Marketing Science*, Fall, pp. 236–244.

Bezos, Jeffrey (1997), "1997 Letters to Shareholders", available at https:// ir.aboutamazon.com/static-files/589ab7fe-9362-4823-a8e5-901f6d3a0f00 (accessed 14 February 2020).

Bezos, Jeffrey (1998), "Letters to Shareholders", available at https:// ir.aboutamazon.com/static-files/4e153845-db22-4ea3-9876-e62b7935 d05e (accessed 14 February 2020).

Bezos, Jeffrey (1999), "Letters to Shareholders", available at https:// ir.aboutamazon.com/static-files/35247dea-9cf4-46e3-9d8e-b501a1e41fee (accessed 14 February 2020).

Bezos, Jeffrey (2000), "Letter to Shareholders", available at https://ir.about amazon.com/annual-reports/ (accessed 5 March 2020).

Bezos, Jeffrey (2001), "Letter to Shareholders", available at https://ir. aboutamazon.com/static-files/b8966f2e-137e-4c10-ac49-e7dfdaac58b4 (accessed 5 March 2020).

Bezos, Jeffrey (2002), "Letters to Shareholders", available at https:// ir.aboutamazon.com/static-files/49eea92e-fdc2-4e41-bf60-f9b8e3b1b133 (accessed 14 February 2020).

Bezos, Jeffrey (2003), "Letters to Shareholders", available at https:// ir.aboutamazon.com/static-files/5383e42d-62c9-4daa-aefb-2887fe5437be (accessed 14 February 2020).

Bezos, Jeffrey (2014), "Letters to Shareholders", available at https://ir.aboutamazon.com/static-files/a9bd5c6a-c11c-4b38-9532-ae2f73d8bd10 (accessed 14 February 2020).

Bezos, Jeffrey (2015), "Letter to Shareholders", available at https://ir.aboutamazon.com/static-files/f124548c-5d0b-41a6-a670-d85bb191f-cec (accessed 5 March 2020).

Bezos, Jeffrey (2018), "Letters to Shareholders", available at https://ir.aboutamazon.com/static-files/4f64d0cd-12f2-4d6c-952e-bbed15ab1082 (accessed 14 February 2020).

Bezos, Jeffrey (letters 1997–2018), "Letters to Shareholders", available at https://ir.aboutamazon.com/annual-reports (accessed 14 February 2020).

Bhattacherjee, Anol (2012), *Social Science Research: Principles, Methods, and Practices*, University of South Florida, Scholar Commons., Tampa, Florida: University of South Florida

Binder, Jochen (2014), *Online Channel Integration: Value Creation and Customer Reactions in Online and Physical Stores*, Wiesbaden: Springer Gabler.

Blakeman, Robin (2018), *Integrated Marketing Communication. Creative Strategy, from Idea to Implementation*, Lanham, MD: Rowman & Littlefield.

Blanchard, Ken (2007), *The Heart of a Leader: Insights on the Art of Influence*, Colorado Springs, CO: David Cook.

Bloomberg Markets and Finance (2018), "YouTube", Amazon CEO Jeff Bezos on The David Rubenstein Show, available at www.youtube.com/watch?v=f3NBQcAqyu4&t=643s (accessed 15 February 2020).

Bough, Victoria Breuer; Ralph Harald Fanderl and Kevin Neher (2017), [McKinsey and Company], "Four Ways to Shape Customer-Experience Measurement for Impact", available at www.mckinsey.com/business-functions/operations/our-insights/four-ways-to-shape-customer-experience-measurement-for-impact (accessed 1 February 2020).

Bowen, Glenn (2009), "Document Analysis as a Qualitative Research Method", *Qualitative Research Journal* Vol. 9, No. 2, pp. 27–40.

Boxwell, Robert (1994), *Benchmarking for Competitive Advantage*, New York, NY: McGraw-Hill Professional Publishing.

Bozeman, Barry and Melkers, Julia (1993), *Evaluating R&D Impacts: Methods and Practice*, Norwell, MA: Kluwer Academic Publishers.

Bracks, Amanda (2012), *Customer Acquisition: 465 Ways to Gain and Retain*, Xlibris Corporation.

Brännback, Malin (1999), "The Concept of Customer-Orientation and Its Implication for Competence Development", INNOMARKET, Turku School of Economics and Business Administration, Department of Marketing, Technical Reports No. 1, May 1999.

Brigham, Eugen and Houston, Joel (2015), *Fundamentals of Financial Management*, Mason, OH: Cengage Learning.

Burns, James (1978), *Leadership*, New York, NY: Open Road Integrated Media.

Burns, James (2003), *Transforming Leadership*, New York, NY: Grove Press.

Butler, Adam (2018), [Forbes], "Do Customers Really Care about Your Environmental Impact?", available at www.forbes.com/sites/forbesny-council/2018/11/21/do-customers-really-care-about-your-environmental-impact/#30ba8cc9240d (accessed 16 December 2019).

Buttle, Francis and Maklan, Stan (2015), *Customer Relationship Management: Concepts and Technologies*, London: Routledge.

Carlyle, Thomas (1840), "On Heroes, Hero-Worship and the Heroic in History", available at www.gutenberg.org/files/1091/1091-h/1091-h.htm (accessed 20 December 2019).

Carrol, Archie and Buchholtz, Ann (2009), *Business & Society: Ethics and Stakeholder Management*, Mason, OH: South-Western Cengage Learning

Chan, Serena (2001), [MIT], "Complex Adaptive Systems", ESD.83 Research Seminar in Engineering Systems, 31 October 2001/6 November 2001, available at http://web.mit.edu/esd.83/www/notebook/Complex%20Adaptive%20Systems.pdf (accessed 9 March 2020).

CIRP (2016), "Amazon Prime Members Stay Members", available at www.cirpllc.com/blog/2017/12/6/amazon-prime-members-stay-members (accessed 29 February 2020).

Clarke, David and Kinghorn, Ron (2018), [PWC], "Experience Is Everything: Here's How to Get It Right", available at www.pwc.com/us/en/advisory-services/publications/consumer-intelligence-series/pwc-consumer-intelligence-series-customer-experience.pdf (accessed 16 January 2020).

Clement, John (2019a), [Statista], "Number of Amazon Prime Members in the United States as of June 2019", available at www.statista.com/statistics/546894/number-of-amazon-prime-paying-members/ (accessed 20 February 2020).

Clement, John (2019b), [Statista], "Amazon Prime - Statistics & Facts", available at www.statista.com/topics/4076/amazon-prime/ (accessed 16 February 2020).

CNBC (2018), [YouTube], Amazon Web Services CEO Andy Jassy on How He Snagged His Dream Job | CNBC, available at www.youtube.com/watch?v=9XTdhpYV168 (accessed 15 February 2020).

CNBC (2019), [YouTube], Watch CNBC's Full Interview with Amazon Worldwide Consumer Chief Jeff Wilke, available at www.youtube.com/watch?v=vcYigkUIi2g (accessed 15 February 2020).

Colon, Alex (2020), [PcMag], "The Best eReaders for 2020", available at www.pcmag.com/roundup/294182/the-best-ebook-readers (accessed 20 February 2020).

Conder, Paul; Bryant, Jake and Meek, Laurie (2014), [Lenati], "The Art and Science of Customer Experience", available at www.lenati.com/wp-content/uploads/legacy/LENATI-THE_ART_AND_SCIENCE_OF_CX.pdf (accessed 9 March 2020).

Connelly, Brian; Certo, Trevis; Ireland, Duane and Reutzel, Christopher (2011), "Signaling Theory: A Review and Assessment", available at http://citeseerx.ist.psu.edu/viewdoc/download?doi=10.1.1.841.5438&rep=rep1&type=pdf (accessed 5 March 2020).

Consumer Policy Research Centre (2017), "Building Customer Trust a Principles and Practice Guide", available at http://cprc.org.au/wp-content/uploads/CPRC_BCTR_WEB.pdf (accessed 20 October 2019).

Couchenour, Donna and Chrisman, J. Kent (2016), *Contemporary Early Childhood Education*, Thousand Oaks, CA: Sage.

de Geus, Arie P. (1998), "The Living Company: A Recipe for Success in the New Economy", available at www.ariedegeus.com/usr/library/documents/main/washingtonquarterly.pdf (accessed 30 December 2019).

Deloitte (2014), "Customer Centricity Embedding It into your Organisation's DNA", available at www2.deloitte.com/content/dam/Deloitte/ie/Documents/Strategy/2014_customer_centricity_deloitte_ireland.pdf (accessed 7 December 2019).

Direct Marketing Association (2014), "Customer Acquisition Barometer 2014. A New Annual Survey of Marketers and Consumers about Acquisition Practices", available at https://dma.org.uk/uploads/customer_aquisition_barometer_2014_report_53d8cf2010a8c.pdf (accessed 16 January 2020).

Drucker, Peter (1986), *Management. Tasks, Responsibilities, Practices*, Toronto: Fitzhenry & Whiteside Ltd.

Drucker, Peter (2008), *Management*, revised edition, New York, NY: HarperCollins e-book.

Eban, Catherine (2019), *Bottle of Lies*, NY: Ecco, an imprint of HarperCollins Publishers, [2019]

Encyclopaedia Britannica (2019a), "Lee Iacocca, American Businessman", available at www.britannica.com/biography/Lee-Iacocca (accessed 28 November 2019).

Encyclopaedia Britannica (2019b), "iPhone. Electronic Device", available at www.britannica.com/technology/iPhone (accessed 30 January 2020).

Ernst & Young (2013), "The Journey toward Greater Customer Centricity", available at www.ey.com/Publication/vwLUAssets/The_journey_toward_greater_customer_centricity/$FILE/Customer_Centricity_Paper_29_April_Final.pdf (accessed 23 October 2019).

Facebook (no data), "Amazon", available at www.facebook.com/Amazon/ (accessed 13 August 2019).

Fader, Peter and Sarah, Toms (2018), *The Customer Centricity Playbook*, Philadelphia, PA: Wharton Digital Press.

Fall, Jaime (2019), [The Amazon blog], "Investing in Education, Training, and Development for Workers", available at https://blog.aboutamazon.com/working-at-amazon/investing-in-education-training-and-development-for-workers (accessed 15 February 2020).

Fan, You; Chen, Cheng and Miao, Lu (2017), "Discussing the Effect of Service Innovation on Customer Satisfaction based on Statistics

Education – A Case on Qianjiangyue Leisure Farm", *EURASIA Journal of Mathematics, Science and Technology Education* Vol. 14, No. 6, pp. 2467–2474.

Fazackerley, Sandra (no data), [LinkedIn], "Fazackerley, Sandra's Personal Page", available at www.linkedin.com/in/sandra-fazackerley-a5383224/?-originalSubdomain=uk (accessed 23 October 2019).

Feedvisor (2019), "The 2019 Amazon Consumer Behavior Report Based on a Survey of 2,000+ U.S. Consumers", available at https://feedvisor.com/resources/amazon-trends/the-2019-amazon-consumer-behavior-report/ (accessed 29 February 2020).

Field, Anne (2008), [Harvard Business Review], "Customer-Focused Leadership", available at https://hbr.org/2008/02/leadership-that-focuses-on-the-1.html (accessed 5 February 2020).

Fisk, Raymond; Grove, Stephen and John, Joby (2014), *Services Marketing Interactive Approach*, Mason, OH: South-Wester, Cengage Learning.

Fisman, Ray and Luca, Michael (2018), [Harvard Business Review], available at https://hbr.org/2018/10/how-amazons-higher-wages-could-increase-productivity (accessed 15 February 2020).

Forbes (2013), "Tips for Building Long-Term Client Relationships", available at www.forbes.com/sites/thesba/2013/04/25/tips-for-building-long-term-client-relationships/#3966cb755567 (accessed 7 December 2019).

Freeman, Edward (2016), "The New Story of Business: Towards a More Responsible Capitalism", a Public Lecture, available at https://onlinelibrary.wiley.com/doi/abs/10.1111/basr.12123 (accessed 6 January 2020).

Freeman, Edward and Dmitriev, Sergiy (2017), "Corporate Social Responsibility and Stakeholder Theory: Learning from Each Other", *SYMPHONYA Emerging Issues in Management* Vol. 1, pp. 7–15.

Freeman, Edward and Velamuri, Ramakrishna (2005), "A New Approach to CSR: Company Stakeholder Responsibility", available at https://papers.ssrn.com/sol3/papers.cfm?abstract_id=1186223 (accessed 18 December 2019).

Fritz, Torsten (2018), [KPMG], "Enabling Voice of the Customer Excellence", available at https://assets.kpmg/content/dam/kpmg/it/pdf/2018/05/enabling-voice-of-the-customer-excellence.pdf (accessed 28 November 2019).

Galar, Diego and Kumar, Uday (2017), *eMaintenance: Essential Electronic Tools for Efficiency*, London: Elsevier, Inc., Academic Press.

Galetto, Molly (2017), [NG DATA], "Customer Retention Marketing: 50 Expert Tips and Insights on Customer Retention Marketing Trends, Tactics and Best Practice Strategies", available at www.ngdata.com/customer-retention-marketing-strategies/ (accessed 15 January 2020).

Gallo, Amy (2014), [*Forbes*], "The Value of Keeping the Right Customers", available at https://hbr.org/2014/10/the-value-of-keeping-the-right-customers (accessed 5 December 2019).

Gallup (2016), "Guide to Customer Centricity Analytics and Advice for B2B Leaders", available at www.gallup.com/ (accessed 16 January 2020).

Gandy, Teresa and Toister, Jeff (2017), "How to Calculate a Customer Satisfaction Score (CSAT)", available at www.callcentrehelper.com/how-to-calculate-customer-satisfaction-csat-109557.htm (accessed 31 January 2020).

Garnet, Kellie (2019), [The Amazon Blog], "5 Things You Don't Know about Safety in Amazon Warehouses", available at https://blog.aboutamazon.com/operations/5-things-you-dont-know-about-safety-in-amazon-warehouses (accessed 19 February 2020).

Gartner (2018), "Realizing the Benefits of Superior Customer Experience: A Gartner Trend Insight Report", available at www.gartner.com/en/doc/3874972-realizing-the-benefits-of-superior-customer-experience-a-gartner-trend-insight-report (accessed 29 December 2019).

Geller, Scott and Veazie, Bob (2017), *The Motivation to Actively Care*, New York, NY: Morgan James Publishing.

Gell-Mann, Murray (1994), "Complex Adaptive Systems", *Sciences of Complexity, Proc.* Vol. XIX, Addison-Wesley, available at https://authors.library.caltech.edu/60491/1/MGM%20113.pdf (accessed 9 March 2020).

General Electric (2017), "GE Additive Opens Customer Experience Center in Munich", available at www.genewsroom.com/press-releases/ge-additive-opens-customer-experience-center-munich (accessed 6 December 2020).

General Electric (2018), "Annual Report", available at www.ge.com/investor-relations/sites/default/files/GE_AR18.pdf (accessed 7 December 2019).

GFK (2017), "Building a Customer Centric Brand by Transforming the Customer Experience", available at www.gfk.com/fileadmin/user_upload/dyna_content/GB/documents/CustomerCentricity_A4.pdf (accessed 16 December 2019).

Giménez, Josep (2018), *Customer-Centricity: The New Path to Product Innovation and Profitability*, Cambridge: Cambridge Scholar Publishing.

Glassdoor (2017), "Do Customers Care How Employees Are Treated?" available at www.glassdoor.com/research/do-customers-care-how-employees-are-treated/ (accessed 16 January 2020).

Glassdoor (2019), Amazon Reviews", available at www.glassdoor.com/Reviews/Amazon-Reviews-E6036.htm (accessed 15 February 2020).

Glassdoor (no data), "Amazon Overview", www.glassdoor.ie/Overview/Working-at-Amazon-EI_IE6036.11,17.htm (accessed 1 March 2020).

Goasduff, Laurence (2019), [Gartner], "As Organizations Strive to become Customer-Centric, "Gartner Identified 10 Common Habits of Organizations Exercising Customer Centricity", available at www.gartner.com/smarterwithgartner/is-your-organization-customer-centric/ (accessed 23 October 2019).

Golding, Ian (2014), "Shareholder or Customer First? The difference between Tesco and Amazon", available at https://ijgolding.com/2014/10/24/shareholder-or-customer-first-the-difference-between-tesco-and-amazon/ (accessed 17 January 2020).

Golding, Ian (2017), [*Customer Experience Magazine*], "The 14 Leadership Principles that Drive Amazon", available at https://cxm.world/14-leadership-principles-drive-amazon/ (accessed 15 February 2020).

UK Government (no data), "National Minimum Wage and National Living Wage Rates", available at www.gov.uk/national-minimum-wage-rates (accessed 15 February 2020).

Gorchels, Linda (2000), *The Product Manager's Handbook. The Complete Product Management Resource*, USA: McGraw-Hill eBooks.

Green, Jay (2015), [*The Seattle Times*], "10 Years Later, Amazon Celebrates Prime's Triumph", available at www.seattletimes.com/business/amazon/10-years-later-amazon-celebrates-primes-triumph/ (accessed 15 February 2020).

Grönroos, Christian and Helle, Pekka (2010), "Adopting a Service Logic in Manufacturing: Conceptual Foundation and Metrics for Mutual Value Creation", *Journal of Service Management* Vol. 21, No. 5, pp. 564–590.

GSM Arena (no data), "Samsung Galaxy Note 7", available at www.gsmarena.com/samsung_galaxy_note7-8082.php (accessed 5 January 2020).

Hamrefors, Sven (2010), "Communicative Leadership. Modern Leadership in Value-Creating Networks", available at http://hamrefors.se/Publikationer/Communicative_Leadership.pdf (accessed 5 February 2020).

Harris, Bonnie (2016), "Top IMC Campaigns of 2015", available at https://prsay.prsa.org/2015/11/02/top-imc-campaigns-of-2015/ (accessed 14 February 2020).

Harvard Analytics Services (2019), *Cultivating Trust to Gain Competitive Advantage. How to Rebuild Confidence in the Way Business is Done*, Cambridge, MA: Harvard Business School Publishing.

Hemel, Carmen and Rademakers, Martijn (2016), "Building Customer-Centric Organization: Shaping Factors and Barriers", *Journal of Creating Value* Vol. 2, No. 2, SAGE publications, pp. 211–230.

Hernandez, Julio (2016), [KPMG], "How Much Is Customer Experience Worth?", available at https://assets.kpmg/content/dam/kpmg/xx/pdf/2016/11/How-much-is-custerom-experience-worth.pdf (accessed 27 November 2019).

Hill, Arthur (2012), *The Encyclopedia of Operations Management: A Field Manual and Glossary of Operations Management Terms and Concepts*, Hoboken, NJ: Pearson Education, Inc.

Hiller, Nathan and Beauchesne, Marie-Michele (2014), "Executive Leadership: CEOs, Top Management Teams, and Organizational-Level Outcomes", in David V. Day (Ed.), *The Oxford Handbook of Leadership and Organizations* (Chapter 30). New York, NY: Oxford University Press.

Hiltz, Mark (2001), *The Marketer's Handbook: A Checklist Approach*, Markcheck Publishing.

Hollader, David; Hertzet, Kaenan and Wassink, Bernhard Klein (2013), [Ernst & Young], "The Journey toward Greater Customer Centricity", available at www.ey.com/Publication/vwLUAssets/The_journey_toward_greater_customer_centricity_-_US/$FILE/Customer_Centricity_Paper_29_April_Final_US.pdf (accessed 28 November 2019).

Hsieh, Tony (2009), [Zappos], "CEO Letter", available at www.zappos.com/ceoletter (accessed 30 December 2019).

Hultgren, Thor (1965), "Cost, Prices, and Profits: Their Cyclical Relations", available at www.nber.org/chapters/c1630.pdf (accessed 1 February 2020).

Hyken, Shep (2018), [Forbes], "Customer Experience is the New Brand", available at www.forbes.com/sites/shephyken/2018/07/15/customer-experience-is-the-new-brand/#65c261557f52 (accessed 31 January 2020).

Interbrand (2018), "Best Global Brands 2018 Rankings", available at www.interbrand.com/best-brands/best-global-brands/2018/ranking/ (accessed 30 January 2020).

Interbrand (2019), "Best Global Brands 2019 Rankings", available at www.interbrand.com/best-brands/best-global-brands/2019/ranking/ (accessed 16 February 2020).

Jackson, Michael (2003), *Systems Thinking: Creative Holism for Managers*, Chichester: John Wiley & Sons Ltd.

Johnson, Michael; Herrmann, Andreas; Frank Huber and Gustafsson, Anders (1997), *Customer Retention in the Automotive Industry: Quality, Satisfaction and Loyalty*, Wiesbaden: Gabler.

Jones, Chris (2012), *The DNA of Collaboration: Unlocking the Potential of 21st Century Teams*, Charlotte, NC: Amberwood Media Group.

Juska, Jerome (2018), *Integrated Marketing Communication: Advertising and Promotion in a Digital World*, New York, NY: Routledge.

Kantor, Jodi and Streitfeld, David (2015), [*The New York Times*], "Inside Amazon: Wrestling Big Ideas in a Bruising Workplace", available at www.nytimes.com/2015/08/16/technology/inside-amazon-wrestling-big-ideas-in-a-bruising-workplace.html (accessed 15 February 2020).

Kelly, Jerry (2018), [Forbes], "How a Customer-Centric Approach Will Help You Win in Business", available at www.forbes.com/sites/forbesagency-council/2018/09/25/how-a-customer-centric-approach-will-help-you-win-in-business/#2c209da02ee5 (accessed 28 November 2019).

Khan, Jawad (no data), [Hiver], "How to Build a Customer Centric Culture in Your Organization", available at https://hiverhq.com/blog/customer-centric-organization/ (accessed 30 December 2019).

Khan, Shahzad (2013), "Determinants of Customer Retention in Hotel Industry", *Journal of Applied Economics and Business*, Vol. 1, No. 3 October, pp. 42–64.

Kim, Chang-Ran and Siddiqui, Zeba (2014), [Reuters], "India's Sun Pharma to Buy Struggling Ranbaxy for $3.2 billion as Daiichi Sankyo Retreats", available at www.reuters.com/article/us-daiichi-sankyo-ranbaxy-sunpharma/indias-sun-pharma-to-buy-struggling-ranbaxy-for-3-2-billion-as-daiichi-sankyo-retreats-idUSBREA3600L20140407 (accessed 15 December 2019).

Kim, Eugene (2018a), "Amazon Employees Start Their Day by Answering a Simple Question about Work", available at www.cnbc.com/2018/03/30/amazon-employee-reaction-to-hr-programs-connections-forte.html (accessed 1 March 2020).

Kim, Eugene (2018b), [CNBC], "Amazon CFO: Advertising Was a 'Key Contributor' to Revenue Growth", available at www.cnbc.com/2018/02/01/amazon-cfo-brian-olsavsky-advertising-key-contributor-to-q4-growth.html (accessed 15 February 2020).

Kim, Eugene (2019), [CNBC], "Amazon's Executive org Chart, Revealed", available at www.cnbc.com/2019/01/23/who-are-amazons-top-executives-2019.html (accessed 15 February 2020).

Kirkham, Elyssa (2017), [Huffspot], "Amazon Prime Day 2015: Best Deals for July 15", available at www.huffpost.com/entry/amazon-prime-day-2015-bes_b_7772202 (accessed 15 February 2020).

Kocher, David (no data), "GE Digital Recognized for Customer First Approach", available at www.ge.com/digital/blog/ge-digital-recognized-customer-first-approach (accessed 2 February 2020).

Kolb, David (1984), *Experiential Learning: Experience as the Source of Learning and Development*, Englewood Cliffs, NJ: Prentice Hall.

Kopp, Brian (2019), [Gartner], "The Future of Employee Monitoring", available at www.gartner.com/smarterwithgartner/the-future-of-employee-monitoring/ (accessed 1 March 2020).

Kotler, Philip (2002), *Marketing Management*, Boston, MA: Pearson Education Limited.

Kotler, Philip and Keller, Kevin (2006), *Marketing Management*, Upper Saddle River, NJ: Pearson Education.

Kotler, Philip and Keller, Kevin (2016), *Marketing Management*, Upper Saddle River, NJ: Pearson Education.

KPMG (2016), [KPMG], "How Much Is Customer Experience Worth?", available at https://assets.kpmg/content/dam/kpmg/xx/pdf/2016/11/How-much-is-custerom-experience-worth.pdf (accessed 1 February 2020).

KPMG (2017a), "Customer First. Creating a Customer Centric Business", available at https://assets.kpmg/content/dam/kpmg/be/pdf/Markets/customer-first.pdf (accessed 23 October 2019), p. 4.

KPMG (2017b), "Customer First. How to Create a Customer Centric Business and Compete in the Digital Age", available at https://assets.kpmg/content/dam/kpmg/au/pdf/2017/customer-first-digital-age.pdf (accessed 3 January 2020).

Kruse, Kevin (2012), [Forbes], "What Is Employee Engagement", available at www.forbes.com/sites/kevinkruse/2012/06/22/employee-engagement-what-and-why/#56f7f2df7f37 (accessed 16 January 2020).

Kulbyte, Toma (2016), [Superoffice], "37 Customer Experience Statistics You Need to Know for 2020", available at www.superoffice.com/blog/customer-experience-statistics/ (accessed 27 November 2019).

Kumar, Piyush (1999), "The Impact of Long-Term Client Relationships on the Performance of Business Service Firms", available at http://citeseerx.ist.psu.edu/viewdoc/download?doi=10.1.1.197.9643&rep=rep1&type=pdf (accessed 20 October 2019).

Kumar, Viswanathan; Petersen, Andrew and Leone, Robert (2007), [Harvard Business Review], "How Valuable Is Word of Mouth?", available at https://hbr.org/2007/10/how-valuable-is-word-of-mouth (accessed 16 January 2020).

Lakshmi, Tatikonda (2013), "The Hidden Costs of Customer Dissatisfaction", *Management Accounting Quarterly* Vol. 14, No. 3, 34 Spring, available at www.imanet.org/-/media/3624cb55dea84e3c8285bbb5b97fe4e4.ashx (accessed 5 March 2020).

Lee, Se Young and Athavaley, Anjali (2017), [Reuters], "Samsung Launches Galaxy S8 and Dreams of Recovery from Note 7", available at www.reuters.com/article/us-samsung-elec-smartphones-idUSKBN17027R (accessed 6 January 2020).

Lemon, Katherine and Verhoef, Peter (2016), "Understanding Customer Experience throughout the Customer Journey", *Journal of Marketing: AMA/MSI* Special Issue, Vol. 80, November, pp. 69–96.

Lesterwunderman.com (2014), "Words", available at www.lesterwunderman.com/words.html (accessed 28 November 2019).

Levitt, Theodore (1960), "Marketing Myopia", *Harvard Business Review*, July–August, pp. 45–56.

Lewis, Robin (2014), [Forbes], "How Apple Neurologically Hooked Its Customers", available at www.forbes.com/sites/robinlewis/2014/09/02/how-apple-neurologically-hooked-its-customers/#708e05e4ff00 (accessed 30 January 2020).

Li, Jing; Konus, Umut; Langerac, Fred and Weggeman, Mathieu (2016), "Customer Channel Migration and Firm Choice: The Effects of Cross-Channel Competition", *International Journal of Electronic Commerce*, available at www.tandfonline.com/doi/full/10.1080/10864415.2016.1204186 (accessed 16 January 2020).

Lichtenstein, Benyamin B.; Uhl-Bien, Mary; Marion, Russ; Seers, Anson; Orton, James Douglas and Schreiber, Craig (2006), "Complexity Leadership Theory: An Interactive Perspective on Leading in Complex Adaptive Systems", *Management Department Faculty Publications* Vol. 8, available at https://digitalcommons.unl.edu/cgi/viewcontent.cgi?referer=https://www.google.com/&httpsredir=1&article=1007&context=managementfacpub (accessed 9 March 2020).

Lopez, Maribel (2017), [Forbes], "Samsung Explains Note 7 Battery Explosions, and Turns Crisis into Opportunity", available at www.forbes.com/sites/maribellopez/2017/01/22/samsung-reveals-cause-of-note-7-issue-turns-crisis-into-opportunity/#1ad476024f12 (accessed 5 January 2020).

Luce, Ivan (2019), "10 Companies That Spent More than $1 billion in Ads So You'd Buy Their Products", available at www.businessinsider.sg/10-biggest-advertising-spenders-in-the-us-2015-7/ (accessed 14 February 2020).

Macgillavry, Kim and Synian, Pa (2016), "Focusing on the Critical Link between Employee Engagement and Customer Centricity at DHL

Freight", available at https://onlinelibrary.wiley.com/doi/abs/10.1002/joe.21680 (accessed 29 December 2019).

Mann, Robert (2014), "Best Practices in Achieving a Customer-Focused Culture", *Benchmarking an International Journal*, July 2007, pp. 482–496.

Markey, Rob and Reichheld, Fred (2013), [Bain and Company], "The Keys to Effective Learning", available at www.bain.com/insights/the-keys-to-effective-learning (accessed 30 December 2019).

Martens, Brian (2001), "The Impact of Leadership in Applying Systems Thinking to Organizations", *Journals ISSS, International Society for the Systems Sciences*, available at http://journals.isss.org/index.php/proceedings55th/article/viewFile/1648/581 (accessed 4 January 2020).

Maslow, Abraham (1970), *Motivation and Personality*, Harper & Row Publishers, Inc., p. 6.

Matyszczyk, Chris (2018), [ZDNET], "Why Do People Want a New iPhone? This Research Gives a Fascinating Clue", available at www.zdnet.com/article/why-do-people-want-a-new-iphone-this-research-gives-a-fascinating-clue/ (accessed 30 January 2020).

McCracken, Harry (2019), "Meet the Woman behind Amazon's Explosive Growth", available at www.fastcompany.com/90325624/yes-amazon-has-an-hr-chief-meet-beth-galetti (accessed 1 March 2020).

McKinsey & Company (2017), "Customer Experience: New Capabilities, New Audiences, New Opportunities", available at www.mckinsey.com/~/media/mckinsey/featured%20insights/customer%20experience/cx%20compendium%202017/customer-experience-compendium-july-2017.ashx (accessed 7 December 2019).

Mone, Sorina-Diana; Pop, Marius and Racolta-Paina, Nicoleta-Dorina (2013), "The 'What' and 'How' of Marketing Performance Management", *Management and Marketing Challenges for the Knowledge Society* Vol. 8, No. 1, pp. 129–146.

Moon, Mariella (2018), "Amazon Warehouse Workers in Europe Stage Protest on Prime Day", available at www.engadget.com/2018/07/16/amazon-spain-germany-poland-prime-day-protest/ (accessed 15 February 2020).

Moore, Susan (2019), [Gartner], "How to Measure Customer Experience", available at www.gartner.com/smarterwithgartner/how-to-measure-customer-experience/ (accessed 31 January 2020).

Morgan, Blake (2015), [Forbes], "Why Everyone at Your Company Should Train in the Contact Center", available at www.forbes.com/sites/blakemorgan/2015/08/03/why-everyone-at-your-company-should-train-in-the-contact-center/#2e67dd4d2f25 (accessed 15 February 2020).

Morgan, Blake (2018a), [Forbes], "How to Build Trust with your Customers", available at www.forbes.com/sites/blakemorgan/2018/06/11/how-to-build-trust-with-your-customers/#57ddd0d61cd3 (accessed 23 October 2019).

Morgan, Blake (2018b), [*Forbes*], "The 10 Most Customer-Obsessed Companies In 2018", available at www.forbes.com/sites/blakemorgan/2018/02/15/the-10-most-customer-obsessed-companies-in-2018/#5111bfec6ba1 (accessed 30 December 2019).

Newman, Daniel (2016), [Forbes], "Organizational Success Starts with an Integrated Customer Experience Model", available at www.forbes.com/sites/danielnewman/2016/07/19/organizational-success-starts-with-an-integrated-customer-experience-model/#7be1a3dc75a7 (accessed 5 January 2017).

Nicholas, John and Steyn, Herman (2012), *Project Management for Engineering, Business and Technology*, New York, NY: Routledge.

Nielsen (2014), "Doing Well by Doing Good", available at www.nielsen.com/us/en/insights/report/2014/doing-well-by-doing-good/ (accessed 5 March 2020).

Nielsen (2018), "Global Consumers Seek Companies that Care about Environmental Issues", available at www.nielsen.com/eu/en/insights/article/2018/global-consumers-seek-companies-that-care-about-environmental-issues/ (accessed 17 January 2020).

Northouse, Peter (2016), *Leadership. Theory and Practice*, Thousand Oaks, CA: Sage Publications.

O'Hara, Susan and Levin, Ginger (2000), [Project Management Institute], Using Metrics to Demonstrate the Value of Project Management. Paper presented at Project Management Institute Annual Seminars & Symposium, Houston, TX. Newtown Square, available at www.pmi.org/learning/library/metrics-demonstrate-value-project-management-485 (accessed 31 January 2020).

Ohtonen, Janne (2015), "Why Revenues Depend on the Customer Experience you Provide?", available at http://customerthink.com/why-revenues-depend-on-the-customer-experience-you-provide/ (accessed 17 January 2020).

Pacific Consulting Group (2018), "Employee Engagement in Customer Experience (CX) Research Report", available at www.pcgfirm.com/ (accessed 18 January 2020).

Paliszkiewicz, Joanna and Klepacki, Bogdan (2013), [ToKnowPress], "Tools of Building Customer Trust", available at www.toknowpress.net/ISBN/978-961-6914-02-4/papers/ML13-426.pdf (accessed 20 October 2019), p. 1287.

Parekh, Jheel (2018), [The Amazon blog], "Empowering Young Minds through Education & Skilling", available at https://blog.aboutamazon.in/in-the-community/empowering-young-minds-through-education-skilling (accessed 5 March 2020).

Parker, Liam (2018), "Budgeting, Unlocking the Keys to Financial Freedom. How to Start Budgeting and Save More, Retire Early, Get Out of Debt and Live a more Fulfilling and Stress-free Life", Kindle edition.

Partington, Richard (2018), [*The Guardian*], "Amazon Raises Minimum Wage for US and UK Employees", available at www.theguardian.com/technology/2018/oct/02/amazon-raises-minimum-wage-us-uk-employees (accessed 15 February 2020).

Panetta, Kassey (2017), [Gartner], "CX Leaders Face New Challenges without Clarity and under Pressure from Executives and Employees", available at www.gartner.com/smarterwithgartner/analysts-answer-what-challenges-exist-in-customer-experience-strategy/ (accessed 23 October 2019).

Peck, Helen; Payn, Adrian; Christopher, Martin and Clark, Moira (2004), *Relationship Marketing. Strategy and Implementation*, Burlington, MA: Elsevier Butterworth- Heinemann.

Pemberton, Chris (2018), [Gartner], "Key Findings from the Gartner Customer Experience Survey", available at www.gartner.com/en/marketing/insights/articles/key-findings-from-the-gartner-customer-experience-survey (accessed 20 October 2019).

Peppers, Don and Rogers, Martha (2011), *Managing Customer Relationships: A Strategic Framework*, Hoboken, NJ: John Willey and Sons, Inc.

Percy, Larry (2014), *Strategic Integrated Marketing Communications*, New York, NY: Routledge.

Persuit, Jeanne and McDowell Marinchak, Christina (2016), *Integrated Marketing Communication: Creating Spaces for Engagement*, Lexington Books.

Pikton, David and Broderik, Amanda (2005), *Integrated Marketing Communications*, Edinburgh: Pearson Education Limited.

Porter, Michael (1990), *Competitive Advantage*, New York, NY: Free Press.

Pourdehnad, John; Wexler, Erica and Wilson, Dennis (2011), "Integrating System Thinking and Design Thinking", *Organizational Dynamics Working Papers. 10*, pp. 1–16.

Prakash, Neeti (2019), "Amazon Employees Strike in Germany for Better Wages and Working Conditions", available at https://peoplesdispatch.org/2019/04/17/amazon-employees-strike-in-germany-for-better-wages-and-working-conditions/ (accessed 15 February 2020).

Procter&Gamble (2003), [Procter&Gamble], "Our Purpose, Values and Principles", available at www.pg.com/translations/pvp_pdf/english_PVP.pdf (accessed 20 October 2019), p. 2.

Procter&Gamble (2019), "Annual Report", available at www.pginvestor.com/Cache/1001256102.PDF?O=PDF&T=&Y=&D=&FID=1001256102&iid=4004124 (accessed 5 January 2020).

Procter&Gamble (no data), "P&G, Suppliers", available at www.pgsupplier.com/en-US (accessed 15, December 2019).

Ramamoorthy, Chitoor (2000), "A Study of the Service Industry – Functions, Features and Control", *IEICE TRANS COMMUN*, Vol. E83-B, #5, May, pp. 885–902.

Rash, Wayne (2017), [eWeek], "Samsung Galaxy S8 Smartphones' Mission Is to Restore Buyer Confidence", available at www.eweek.com/mobile/samsung-galaxy-s8-smartphones-mission-is-to-restore-buyer-confidence (accessed 6 January 2020).

Reebok (no data), "Be More Human", available at www.reebok.com/us/search?q=be%20more%20human (accessed 4 December 2020).

Redbord, Michael (2018), [The GRI Marketing Group], "The Hard Truth about Acquisition Costs (and How Your Customers Can Save You)", available at www.gridirect.com/clients/GRI_Acquisition_costs.pdf (accessed 5 December 2019).

Reichheld, Fred (2001), [BAIN], "Prescription for Cutting Costs", available at www2.bain.com/Images/BB_Prescription_cutting_costs.pdf (accessed 23 October 2019).

Reputation Institute (2017), "The 2017 Global RepTrak® 100", available at www.reputationinstitute.com/research/2017-global-reptrak (accessed 16 December 2019).

Reuters (2013), "Ranbaxy Pleads Guilty, to Pay $500 mln. in Settlement", available at https://in.reuters.com/article/ranbaxy-settlement-felony-usa-idINDEE94C0DA20130513 (accessed 15 December 2019).

Saeed, Muhammad Sajid (2016), "Obtaining a Sustainable Competitive Advantage through Innovative Marketing Strategies", *Developing Country Studies* Vol. 6, No. 6, pp. 112–118

Saleem, Asma; Ghafar, Abdul; Ibrahim, Muhammad; Yousuf, Muhammad and Ahmed, Naveed (2015), "Product Perceived Quality and Purchase Intention with Consumer Satisfaction", *Global Journal of Management and Business Research: E Marketing* Vol. 15, No. 1, Version 1.0, pp. 21–27.

Samsung (2016), "Business Report", available at https://images.samsung.com/is/content/samsung/p5/global/ir/docs/170331_2016_Business_Report_vF.pdf (accessed 20 October 2019), p. 50.

Samsung (2017), "Samsung Electronics Sustainability Report", available at www.samsung.com/us/smg/content/dam/samsung/us/aboutsamsung/2017/Samsung_Electronics_Sustainability_Report-2017.pdf (accessed 20 October 2019).

Sarabjit Singh Baveja, Sharad Rastogi and Chris, Zook (no data), [BAIN], "The Value of Online Customer Loyalty and How You Can Capture It", available at www2.bain.com/Images/Value_online_customer_loyalty_you_capture.pdf (accessed 6 December 2019).

Sassen, Earl and Arbeit, Stephen (1976), "Selling Jobs in the Service Sector", available at http://web.a.ebscohost.com.ergo.southwales.ac.uk/ehost/pdfviewer/pdfviewer?vid=2&sid=d0ce40f5-8185-4494-a728-27f9580ef-b81%40sdc-v-sessmgr02 (accessed 18 December 2019).

Savitz, Eric (2011), [Forbes], "The New Art and Science of Great Customer Experience", available at www.forbes.com/sites/ciocentral/2011/06/30/the-new-art-and-science-of-great-customer-experience/#5d1522542f90 (accessed 9 March 2020).

Schleifer, Theodore (2020), "Jeff Bezos Just made One of the Largest Charitable Gifts Ever", available at www.vox.com/recode/2020/2/17/21141229/jeff-bezos-climate-change-ten-billion (accessed 5 March 2020).

Schmidt-Subramanian, Maxie; Manning, Harley; Burns, Megan; Czarnecki, Dylan and Hartig, Kara (2016), [Forrester], "Seven Steps to Successful Customer Experience Measurement Programs", available at www10.confirmit.com/rs/107-XEL-280/images/Forrester%20-%20Seven%20Steps%20to%20Successful%20Customer%20Experience%20Measurement%20Programs.pdf (accessed 16 December 2019).

Selden, Larry and MacMillan, Ian (2006), [Harvard Business Review], "Manage Customer-Centric Innovation—Systematically", available at https://hbr.org/2006/04/manage-customer-centric-innovation-systematically (accessed 31 January 2020).

Senge, Peter (2004), *The Fifth Discipline. The Art and Practice of the Learning Organization*, New York, NY: Currency Doubleday.

Severance, Chuck (no data), [YouTube], "Jeff Bezos 1997 Interview" [YouTube], available at www.youtube.com/watch?v=rWRbTnE1PEM (accessed 15 February 2020).

Sexton, Andrew (2013), [LesterWunderman], "Press Kit", available at www.lesterwunderman.com/about.html (accessed 28 November 2019).

Sheth, Jagdish and Sisodia, Rajendra (2012), *The 4 A's of Marketing: Creating Value for Customers, Companies and Society*, New York, NY: Routledge.

Shimp, Terence (2010), *Advertising Promotion and Other Aspects of Integrated Marketing Communications*, Mason, OH: South-Western Cengage Learning.

Shah, Denish; Rust, Roland; Parasuraman, A.; Staelin, Richard and Day, George (2006), "The Path to Customer Centricity", *Journal of Service Research* Vol. 9, p. 113.

Shim, Jae; Siegel, John and Shim, Alisson (2012), "Budgeting Basics and Beyond", 4th edition, available at https://onlinelibrary.wiley.com/doi/book/10.1002/9781118387023 (accessed 31 January 2020).

Shultz, Don; Tannenbaum, Stanley and Lautenborn, Robert (1993), *Integrated Marketing Communications: Putting It Together & Making It Work*, Lincolnwood: NTC Business Books.

Shultz, Don Edward and Kitchen, Philipp (1997), "Integrated Marketing Communications in U.S. Advertising Agencies: An Exploratory Study", *Journal of Advertising Research* Vol. 7, No. 5, pp. 7–18.

Smith, P.R. and Zook, Ze (2011), *Marketing Communications Integrating Offline and Online with Social Media*, London: Kogan Page Limited.

Smith, Adam (2018, originally published in 1776), *The Wealth of Nations*, Global Grey ebooks.

Statista (2018), "Share of Mobile Phone Sales Profit by Vendor Worldwide from 2016 to 2018", available at www.statista.com/statistics/780367/global-mobile-handset-profit-share-by-vendor/ (accessed 30 January 2020).

Statista (2018), "Global Market Share Held by Leading Smartphone Vendors from 4th Quarter 2009 to 3rd Quarter 2019", available at www.statista.com/statistics/271496/global-market-share-held-by-smartphone-vendors-since-4th-quarter-2009/ (accessed 30 January 2020).

Statista (2019), "Net Sales of the Reebok Brand Worldwide from 2006 to 2018", available at www.statista.com/statistics/268422/net-sales-of-the-reebok-brand-worldwide-since-2006/ (accessed 4 December 2020).

Statista (2020), "Customer Churn Rate in the United States in 2018, by Industry", available at www.statista.com/statistics/816735/customer-churn-rate-by-industry-us/ (accessed 15 January 2020).

Stevens, Laura (2017), [The Wall Street Journal], "Jeff Wilke: The Amazon Chief Who Obsesses over Consumers", available at www.wsj.com/articles/jeff-wilke-the-amazon-chief-who-obsesses-over-consumers-1507627802 (accessed 15 February 2020).

Stevenson, William (2015), *Operations Management*, 12th edition, New York, NY: McGraw-Hill Education.

Subramanian, Kalpathy (2017), "Building Customer Relationship through Direct Marketing", *International Journal of Combined Research & Development (IJCRD)* Vol. 6, No. 9, September, pp. 799–810

Subramanian, Kalpathy (2018), "The Connection between your Employees and Customers", *Journal of Advance Research in Business Management and Accounting* Vol. 4, No. 8, pp. 1–14.

Tate, Andrew (2020), [ProfitWell], "How to Calculate Customer Churn Rate (+the best SAAS Churn Formula)", available at www.profitwell.com/blog/the-complete-saas-guide-to-calculating-churn-rate-and-keeping-it-simple (accessed 16 January 2020).

Taylor, |James (2014), "Real-Time Responses with Big Data", available at www.oracle.com/assets/realtime-responses-big-data-wp-2524527.pdf (accessed 31 January 2020).

Tesco-Careers (no data), "Everyone Is Welcome", available at www.tesco-careers.com/explore-our-world/everyone-is-welcome/ (accessed 17 January 2020).

Tesco (2016), "Annual Report and Financial Statements 2016", available at www.tescoplc.com/media/264194/annual-report-2016.pdf (accessed 20 October 2019).

Tesco (2017a), "Annual Report and Financial Statements 2017", available at www.tescoplc.com/media/392373/68336_tesco_ar_digital_interactive_250417.pdf (accessed 20 October 2019).

Tesco (2017b), [TESCO], "Customers, Product, Channels", available at www.tescoplc.com/media/392340/tesco_ar17_businessmodel.pdf (accessed 20 October 2019).

Tesco (2018), [TESCO], "Annual Report and Financial Statements 2018", available at www.tescoplc.com/media/474793/tesco_ar_2018.pdf (accessed 20 October 2019).

Tesco (2019), "Annual Report and Financial Statements 2017", available at www.tescoplc.com/media/476422/tesco_ara2019_full_report_web.pdf (accessed 17 January 2020).

Tesla (no data), "Advancing Automotive Service", available at www.tesla.com/en_IE/service (accessed 7 December 2019).

The Amazon blog (2019), "The History of Prime Day", available at https://blog.aboutamazon.com/shopping/the-history-of-prime-day#target Text=Prime%20Day%202015%20highlights&targetText=%2D%20 They%20ordered%2034.4%20million%20items, device%20sales%20 day%20ever%2C%20worldwide (accessed 14 February 2020).

The Amazon blog (no data), "Compensation and Benefits", available at www.aboutamazon.com/amazon-fulfillment/working-here/compensation-and-benefits (accessed 15 February 2020).

The Amazon blog (no data), "Corporate Governance", available at https://ir.aboutamazon.com/corporate-governance (accessed 5 March 2020).

The Amazon blog (no data), "Engagement in Our Communities", available at www.aboutamazon.de/logistikzentrum/lokale-investitionen/engagement-in-unseren-gemeinden (accessed 5 March 2020).

The Amazon Jobs (no data), "Leadership Principles", available at www.amazon.jobs/en/principles (accessed 15 February 2020).

The Amazon blog (no data), "Officers and Directors", available at https://ir.aboutamazon.com/board-of-directors (accessed 15 February 2020).

The Amazon blog (no data), "Our Upskilling 2025 Programs", available at www.aboutamazon.com/working-at-amazon/upskilling-2025/our-upskilling-2025-programs (accessed 15 February 2020).

The Amazon blog (2020), "Every Dollar Helps", available at https://blog.aboutamazon.com/community/every-dollar-helps (accessed 5 March 2020).

The Amazon blog (2020), "Powering HQ2 with 100% Renewable Energy", available at https://blog.aboutamazon.com/search?q=renewable+energy (accessed 5 March 2020).

Tracy, John (2002), *The Fast Forward MBA in Finance*, New York, NY: John Wiley & Sons, Inc.

TripAdvisor (no data), "GoPro", available at www.tripadvisor.com/Profile/GoPro?fid=905d612b-0d71-4fe4-a233-4ce63ce4dbb7 (accessed 16 December 2019).

Tsukayama, Hayley (2017), [The Washington Post], "Samsung Tries to Reclaim Its Reputation with the Galaxy S8", available at www.reuters.com/article/us-samsung-elec-smartphones-idUSKBN17027R (accessed 6 January 2020).

Twitter (no data), "GoPro", available at https://twitter.com/gopro?lang=en (accessed 16 December 2019).

Twitter (no data), "Amazon", available at https://twitter.com/amazon?ref_src=twsrc%5Egoogle%7Ctwcamp%5Eserp%7Ctwgr%5Eauthor (accessed 13 August 2019).

Vader, Rene (2018), [KPMG], "Customer Centricity. Getting It Right Is Hard – but Essential", available at https://home.kpmg/xx/en/home/insights/2018/06/top-of-mind-2018-customer-centricity.html (accessed 20 October 2019).

Vance, Robert (2006), *Employee Engagement and Commitment A Guide to Understanding, Measuring and Increasing Engagement in your Organization*, Alexandria, VA: SHRM Foundation.

Variyar, Mudha (2018), [Economic times], "Amazon Wages in Step with Rivals in India", available at https://economictimes.indiatimes.com/smallbiz/startups/newsbuzz/amazon-wages-in-step-with-rivals-in-india/articleshow/66079573.cms?from=mdr (accessed 15 February 2020).

Veber, Max (1964), *The Theory of Social and Economic Organization*, New York, NY: The Free Press.

Verhage, Bronis (2013), *Marketing Fundamentals. An International Perspective*, The Netherlands: Noordhoff Uitgevers.

Walker (2013), [Walker info], "Customers. The Future of Customer Experience. 2020", available at www.walkerinfo.com/Portals/0/Documents/Knowledge%20Center/Featured%20Reports/WALKER-Customers2020.pdf (accessed 23 October 2019).

Weinstein, Art and Elison, Hank (2012), *Superior Customer Value: Strategies for Winning and Retaining Customers*, Boca Raton, FL: CRC Press Taylor & Francis group.

Welch, Jack and Welch, Suzi (2005), *Winning*, New York, NY: Harper Collins Publishers.

Wenger, Etienne (1998), "Communities of Practice: Learning, Meaning, and Identity", *Journal of Mathematics Teacher Education* Vol. 6, No. 2, June 2003, pp. 185–194.

Wenger, Etienne (2006), "Communities of Practice a Brief Introduction", available at www.scribd.com/document/65526908/Communities-of-Practice-A-Brief-Introduction (accessed 30 December 2019), pp. 1–5.

Wenger-Trayner, Etienne and Wenger-Trayner, Beverly (2015), "Introduction to Communities of Practice. A Brief Overview of the Concept and Its Uses", available at https://wenger-trayner.com/introduction-to-communities-of-practice/ (accessed 30 December 2019).

Whitler, Kimberly (2014), "Why Word of Mouth Marketing Is the Most Important Social Media", available at www.forbes.com/sites/kimberlywhitler/2014/07/17/why-word-of-mouth-marketing-is-the-most-important-social-media/#1f4efebf54a8 (accessed 16 January 2020).

Whitley, Margaret (2006), *Leadership and the New Science: Discovering Order in a Chaotic World*, San Francisco, CA: Barret Koehler Publishers, Inc.

Wiles, Jackie (2018), [Gartner], "9 Questions That Should Be in Every Employee Engagement Survey", available at www.gartner.com/smarterwithgartner/the-9-questions-that-should-be-in-every-employee-engagement-survey/ (accessed 1 February 2020).

Wilke, Jeff (2019), [Amazon], "Amazon's Impact on Small Businesses", available at https://blog.aboutamazon.com/small-business/amazons-impact-on-small-businesses (accessed 4 March 2019).

Wunderman, Lester (1998), *Being Direct: Making Advertising Pay*, New York, NY: Random House.

Yahoo finance (2020), Amazon.com, Inc. (AMZN), available at https://finance.yahoo.com/quote/AMZN/ (accessed 15 February 2020).

Yohn, Denis (2018a), [Forbes], "The Secret to Superior Customer Experience", available at www.forbes.com/sites/deniselyohn/2018/04/18/the-secret-to-superior-customer-experience/#713d20ff1f2c (accessed 17 January 2020).

Yohn, Denis (2018b), "6 Ways to Build a Customer-Centric Culture", available at https://hbr.org/2018/10/6-ways-to-build-a-customer-centric-culture (accessed 30 December 2017).

YouTube (no data), "GoPro", available at www.youtube.com/user/GoPro-Camera/about (accessed 16 December 2019).

YouTube (no data), "Amazon", available at www.youtube.com/user/amazon (accessed 13 August 2019).

Zafer, Alkhatani Saad (2015), *Authentic Customer Centricity*, Charlotte, NC: Information Age Publishing, Inc.

Zappos (no data), "What We Live By", available at www.zappos.com/about/what-we-live-by6 (accessed 30 December 2019).

Zappos (no data), "How We Work", available at www.zappos.com/about/how-we-work (accessed 30 December 2019).

Zhang, Yan (2019), [*Forbes*], "Three Highly Effective Strategies of Customer Acquisition Marketing", available at www.forbes.com/sites/forbesagencycouncil/2019/01/04/three-highly-effective-strategies-of-customer-acquisition-marketing/#1c7293714da6 (accessed 16 January 2020).

Zorfas, Alan and Leemon, Daniel (2016), [*Forbes*], "An Emotional Connection Matters More than Customer Satisfaction", available at https://hbr.org/2016/08/an-emotional-connection-matters-more-than-customer-satisfaction (accessed 30 January 2020).

Index

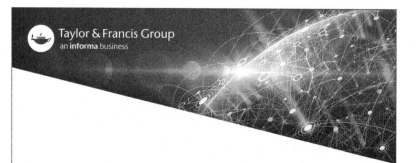

Printed in the United States
by Baker & Taylor Publisher Services